the
American Blues

Also by Ward Just

Ward Just

the American Blues

The Viking Press
New York

Chapter One and portions of Chapter Two of this book appeared originally in
TriQuarterly magazine, a publication of Northwestern University.

Library of Congress Cataloging in Publication Data
Just, Ward S.
The American blues.
I. Title.
PS3560.U75A8   1984   813'.54   83-40224
ISBN 0-670-11712-9

Grateful acknowledgment is made to the following for permission to reprint
copyrighted material:

Southern Music Publishing Co., Inc.: A selection from "You've Changed," by
Bill Carey and Carl Fischer. Copyright 1942, 1943 and 1947 by Melody Lane
Publications, Inc. Copyrights renewed by Melody Lane Publications, Inc., and
Southern Music Publishing Co., Inc. All rights reserved.

Viking Penguin Inc.: A selection from *Black Lamb and Grey Falcon,* by Rebecca
West. Copyright 1940, 1941 by Rebecca West. Copyright renewed 1968, 1969
by Rebecca West.

Printed in the United States of America
Set in Clarendon light

To Sarah

Idiocy is the female defect: intent on their private lives, women follow their fate through a darkness deep as that cast by malformed cells in the brain. It is no worse than the male defect, which is lunacy: they are so obsessed by public affairs that they see the world as by moonlight, which shows the outlines of every object but not the details indicative of their nature.

—Rebecca West, *Black Lamb and Grey Falcon*

the
American Blues

one

This is not a story of the war, except insofar as everything in my unsettled middle age seems to wind back to it. I know how much you dislike reading about it, all dissolution, failure, hackneyed ironies, and guilt, not to mention the facts themselves, regiments of them, *armies*. But I must risk being the bore at dinner for these few opening pages, for the life of the war is essential to the story I have to tell. And that is not about the war at all but about the peace that followed the war.

At the time the People's Army commenced its final murderous assault on Saigon I was living safely in a remote district of New England, far from the anarchy of battle and outside the circulation zones of serious newspapers. This was several years after my wife and I had quit the city for the country, having decided to go back to basics in the woods. We wanted a natural environment, clean air, safe schools, wood stoves, and a preindustrial economy. In our fervor to simplify, we went to the northern edge of the nation, thinking of it as the frontier.

In fact, we were refugees from wartime Washington. Or perhaps the more accurate term is exiles, though no one forced us to leave. Our exile was voluntary: we abandoned Washington as good soldiers might desert a ravaging army.

We believed that our home for many years had become dis-
eased—poisoned with greed, ambition, and bloodlust. My
wife saw this before I did, and saw also that we had become
part of it, accomplices—against our will, she insisted, though
of course as a journalist I had been a willing witness to the
war's progress, drawn to it for no other reason than it was
there, remaining because there seemed no other place to be.
In Washington my wife and I feared for what we considered
our special closeness and appetite for each other. Sexual
passion withered in the heat of such megalomania. My wife
thought of the capital as some monstrous contagion, hence
our abrupt and bravura departure for the north country—
from the vicious to the chaste, from the extraneous to the
basic, from the heart of America to its margins. This was
in 1973.

Without newspapers to read, I followed the end of the
war on television, via a single network, because my house
was so situated in the mountains that I could receive only
one channel. I watched the collapse on that one network,
my continuity. And it was different from yours. I knew the
theater of operations, its geography and ambience, and many
of the American officials present at the end and most of
the journalists. I knew its history as well as I knew my
own, having been there for two and half years, and indeed
in some respects watching the war on television was like
watching a home movie, a blurred 8mm film from childhood
showing the house we no longer lived in and the father who
was dead, a tiresome experience unless you had been there
and remembered: then it was excruciating. This was a house
in which some part of you would always dwell and a father
who would be on guard forever. You saw yourself skylarking, innocent, and unafraid, though entirely aware of the
Kodak whirring away, seizing the moment. I wanted to call
out and stop the film: *Don't Do That!* But it would speed up,
the images racing, faster and faster, and there was no stopping it, then or later. Of course at the time the future was
unrevealed: I could not foresee the consequences. Later, I

would understand that it was predictable—even by me, one who believed that history never repeated itself. What came later was no surprise, including my own broken nerves and trepidation. The shakes came much later, when images leached from my memory like shrapnel from flesh: so many human beings, multitudes. I had watched them, now they watched me; turn, and turn about. In 1975 it was my own memory on film, and this memory was crowded with fear and ardor, hot and bittersweet as an old blues,

> You told me that you loved me
> but you told me a lie.

They were diabolical memories, hard to communicate and ever harder to share. Yet my feet beat perfect time to the music, everyone said so. The war, the war, the war, the war; for a while, we thought it would go on forever, a running story. And how fascinating that it was an American responsibility, supervised by our best minds. Surely somewhere there was consolation.

So I leaned forward toward the small screen, connected to the war by the network, my looking glass. I was alert to the most obscure detail, often smiling, frequently near tears. It was all personal. I knew their faces, mannerisms, and personal histories. A particular friend of mine was a senior diplomat in the American embassy who was routinely interviewed in the last days by my old colleague Nicholson. The interviews were near parodies of the decades-old quarrel between officials and reporters. My friend was by then a very tired and distracted official, and he gave Nicholson no satisfaction. Of course Nick was polite and sympathetic, his bedside manner never more attractive than when tending a terminally ill patient. But my friend gave at least as good as he got, and his truculence amid the ruins showed him to good advantage. On the small screen he was a formidable character.

Nicholson asked him, "What do you think, now that it's almost over?"

3

My friend was shrewdly silent, knowing that television cannot abide silence. He was careful not to move his eyes or dip his head or otherwise display embarrassment or disarray.

Annoyed, Nicholson began again. "It's collapsing all along the line." He named the provincial capitals that had fallen in the past twenty-four hours, even pretty little My Tho was under siege. "And now that it is. Is there something we could have done differently? Or should have or might have? Or perhaps there was something we shouldn't've done at all?" Nicholson leaned over my friend's gunmetal desk, holding the microphone delicately with his thumb and forefinger, as he might a flute of champagne. He scented blood.

My friend said, "Yes," not needing to add "you son of a bitch," because it was plain in the tone of his voice. They had known and cordially disliked each other for years.

Nicholson said, "Looking back on it—"

"Looking back on it is something we'll do for a very long time," my friend said. "It'll become an industry. There are so many of us who've been here."

"Yes," Nick said. The camera moved in tight on him. "And the lessons? What will the lessons be?"

"In order to sleep soundly, Americans will believe anything. Do you know who said that?"

Nicholson, thrown on the defensive, shook his head.

"Stalin," my friend said.

"Well—"

"According to Shostakovich." Nick said nothing, wary now and alert to diplomatic nuance. But my friend only added mildly, "The composer. In his memoirs, I think."

Nick pounced: "But what will they *be*, the lessons?"

The diplomat's voice was soft, almost hushed. "They will be whatever makes us think well of ourselves. So that our sleep will be untroubled. But it's too early to tell, isn't it? We must wait for the after-action reports. The conferences and symposia. The publication of classified docu-

4

ments." I watched my friend thrust and parry, his face perfectly expressionless, though drawn. I thought he was getting the better of it.

"You've been here as long as anyone," Nicholson said, smiling as if he intended a compliment. "And now you seem to be saying that the war's ended at last." Nick wanted a confession and this was by way of reading the subject his rights. He moved the microphone in the direction of the window and cocked his head, smiling wanly. Boom boom. Gunfire, or what sounded like gunfire.

"It is lost, yes."

"That's not the same thing," Nicholson said.

"No," my friend agreed.

"Well!" Nicholson said, smiling again. I noticed that he had had his teeth capped. He looked fit, though tired. Probably it was only a hangover. "Surely you would not contend—"

"I am not contending anything," my friend said. "It's only a word. Pick the word you want. Your word isn't accurate, as a matter of fact. The war will not end when the Americans leave. One part of the war will end but the war has more than one part. However, this is not our happiest or our proudest or our most honorable hour. If that is what you want me to say, I am saying it." He opened his mouth as if to continue, then didn't. He probably figured he had said too much. There was a moment of silence. Nicholson let it run, knowing now that the advantage was his. My friend said, "One can choose his own word. That word or some other word. It depends on where one sits."

Lame, I thought. Dour, obscure, and unconvincing. But dead accurate.

"Right now," Nick said smoothly, "we're sitting in the American embassy, third floor." He smiled again and gestured at the American flag behind the big desk. It hung from a standard crowned with a fierce golden American eagle. There were framed documents on the walls, and a lithograph that I remembered from other occasions. My friend took it with him wherever he went, one of Picasso's melancholy musicians. The camera lingered on it.

"Exactly," my friend said. His voice was like flint, and now he moved to gather some papers on his desk. He ignored the microphone Nick held only inches from the end of his nose. "At least you've got that exactly right, where we are now."

I remembered his tone of voice from another occasion, early in the war. He had taken me to lunch to explain a particularly subtle turn in American war diplomacy. It was too subtle for me, I didn't get any of it, but I did not let on and let him talk himself out, thinking that sooner or later I would pick it up, understand what it was he was trying to tell me, and then I would have a story. He wound down at last and looked at me with a frigid smile. Then he said, "It's convenient for you, isn't it? Being here, listening to me, waiting for a crumb of information. Some fact, any fact at all will do, so long as it's fresh. Facts and fish stink after a day in this heat. Isn't that right?" I protested. It was *his* lunch, undertaken at *his* invitation—Yes, he said wearily, that was true. Then he laughed, and when I asked him what was funny, he replied that his situation was too droll; now he was conducting diplomacy through the newspapers, and they were American newspapers. He explained that he was trying to reach a certain circle in Washington, and he thought he could do it through my newspaper, through me. They never read the cables, and when they did they carped and complained. . . . Too droll, he said again, ordering cognacs for us both; it wasn't diplomacy at all, it was public relations.

There was a brief fade to black and then the camera went in tight on Nicholson. Now he was standing in the embassy driveway. He delivered a few portentous sentences, a kind of fatigued now-you-see-it-now-you-don't commentary on the interview. Artillery crashed in the background. Then he identified himself, "outside the American embassy on Thong Nhat Avenue, Saigon."

6

Nicholson had a reputation as television's most adroit interviewer, but that was the closest he came to cracking my friend. And he kept at it, night after night. Their little sparring match would end Nick's report, until more violent events in the streets made interviews superfluous, or perhaps they both tired of the charade. I admired my friend's tenacity but I was distressed at his appearance, his eyes tired and his hair graying and longer than I remembered it, his widow's peak pronounced and causing him to look older than he was. His shaggy hair gave him an untidy appearance. Normally he was a fastidious man and a model diplomat, the son of one ambassador and the nephew of another, the grandson of an army general and the great-grandson of a secretary of the treasury. One way and another his family had been in government for a hundred years, and this fact was never very far from my friend's thoughts, certainly not then, in the last days of the war. Despite his ancestry, or because of it, he was the most "European" of the American officials I knew. His was a layered, mordant personality, the past and the present always in subtle play. He had married and divorced a Parisian and was now married to an Italian woman, a Venetian who was my wife's closest friend; my wife and the Venetian had studied history together. He had a special affection for his wife's family who had survived, by his estimate, seven centuries of criminal venery from the doges to Mussolini, in the family palazzo on the Grand Canal—and how had they survived? Indolence, he said.

I pulled for the diplomat in his struggle with Nicholson, and not only because of my friendship with him and my wife's with his languid Venetian lady. I wanted to see him come away with something. There was no equity in an agony where only the observers profited. The more bad news the better, the deeper the quagmire the more the correspondents flourished. Connoisseurs of bad news, Nicholson and I had been the most celebrated of the virtuosos, Nick with his camera and deft interrogation and I with my pencil and notebook and clear sight. We were scrupulous in our search for delusion, error, and falsehood. We worked close to the fire, give us that; and we were entranced by its light, smitten, infatuated. And it was not a schoolboy's crush but a grand passion, a *coup de foudre* that often strikes men of a certain age. However, my mordant friend was not smitten, and he distrusted romantic metaphors. He believed simply that the United States had gotten itself into a war that it could not win. It could not win against the Vietnamese Communists any more than Bonaparte could win against the Russian winter. Americans had begun the war with an excess of optimism, but what country did not? The Italians always had. Now there would be consequences and to avoid them would only make matters worse, perhaps a good deal worse. Of course he hated being a part of it, there had been so many blunders and so many dead and so much waste. And unlike the Italians, we had tried so hard.

In front of the camera my friend was still and contained and vaguely contemptuous. He approved of journalism in the abstract but disliked the kind of man who seemed attracted to it. Journalists seemed to him to be naïve utopians, and they were never worse than when covering wars. They routinely violated the physicist's great rule, "Everything should be made as simple as possible, but not simpler." And Nicholson and I? We tried hard, too; no one could fault our zeal. Our enthusiasm for the fall—its blood and dark rhythms, its delusion, the inexorability of the descent, the fulfillment of all the worst prophecies—was almost religious in its intensity, and at home our dispatches were followed with the devotion that Gypsies give tarots. Of course we wanted no wider war, Nicholson and I—though I was obsessed with my friend's prediction, it seemed almost to be a curse: "Now there will be consequences and to avoid them would only make things worse, perhaps a good deal worse."

That was my own situation, appallingly real in the

north country as I watched my friend on the small screen. He was a good man and an able diplomat and I felt sorry for him, distressed at his appearance and uncomfortable in his company, though we were twelve thousand miles apart; and of course disappointed that he never looked the camera in the eye, though that may have been the strategy of the cameraman, who had been with Nicholson for many years. Nick was a professional, no more but no less either.

◇

That last week of the war I watched television every day, beginning with the morning news and ending with the wrap-up at eleven. Of course I was most attentive in the evening, my own day done; and knowing that in the Zone it was early morning. Their day was just beginning. Each day was worse than the day before, and the suspense was in wondering how much worse. How bad could it get? My wife refused to watch with me, being opposed both to the war and to television news on principle. We had always been great newspaper readers. In the evenings my son, aged seven, agreed to keep me company. That last week there was combat footage from the countryside and film also of the various landmarks in the capital, the Street of Flowers, the old JUSPAO building, Aterbea's Restaurant, the National Assembly, and the two white hotels, the Caravelle and the Continental, all places I knew well from the previous decade.

Don't you want to see this? I called to my wife.

Not especially, she said from the kitchen.

Look, I said, there's Jessel. This was another old friend, a newspaperman. A hand-held camera caught him standing in Lam Son Square at the corner of the rue Catinat, making notes. He was wearing a sort of bush suit and a side arm in a holster and a steel helmet. He was thick around the middle.

I don't know him, she said.

I said, Sure you do, don't you remember? We met him

9

and his wife, his then-wife, in New York that time. That time we had so much fun in the bar at the Algonquin. She was very young. You liked his wife, remember?

She said, Yes. It was at some bar. And they're divorced now. And I didn't like her.

I said, I wish to hell they didn't wear those bush suits. They didn't wear them in my day, at least the newspapermen didn't. And, Christ, he's packing heat. He thinks he's Ernest Hemingway, liberating the bar of the Caravelle. Except he's not going in, he's going out.

My son squirmed on the couch next to me.

I think it's a violation of the Geneva Convention, I continued. The rules are very clear. Correspondents are not combatants, and they are not authorized to bear arms. And you have the rank of major, so if you're captured you're a field-grade officer and entitled to respect—

Your dinner's ready, she said.

In a minute, I replied. I was watching Jessel, so tubby and complacent. In the old days Jessel had never worn bush suits. The war was not a safari. He had never carried a handgun, either.

I'll go ahead then, she said.

A rooftop shot from the Caravelle restaurant provoked a cascade of reminiscence, much of it overwrought, perhaps bogus. This lunch, that dinner; who was present and what we ate and the details of the winelist, and the horror stories, the changing estimate of the situation, and the waiter whom we believed to be a VC agent. A glimpse of the adjoining building made me laugh out loud. It was the apartment window of the Indian money changer, the "mahatma"; the window was ablaze with light, and I imagined the transactions within, tortuous now no doubt. I described the look of the flares over the Mekong, the river bright as a carnival in the light of burning phosphorus, and the thump of artillery on the opposite shore. I was being cheerful for the benefit of my wife, who had convinced herself that we had all had a fine time in South Vietnam.

10

I thought again of Jessel. At that time he was living with a Vietnamese woman with whom he had no common language. His American girlfriend, the young woman he later married, had gone home. The Vietnamese was a well-educated woman who spoke excellent French, but Jessel had no French, so they communicated by high sign and in pigeon.

Jessel, I said. A funny son of a bitch.

Then a radio jingle came back to me, a choir:

> Don't you get a little lonely
> All by yourself
> Out on that limb?
> Without Him?

The last word was drawn out, in barbershop harmony, Himmmmmmmm. Sponsored by the Army chaplain corps, it ran a dozen times a day on the Armed Forces Radio Network, inserted between the Supremes and Jimi Hendrix and exhortations to Stay Alert, Stay Alive. I sang the jingle to my son, who did not understand it. I remembered smiling every time I heard it. It was so—chaste. And the chaplains were so demoralized and broken up. They were from another world altogether, and now, thinking about them and their jingle, I moved to the other end of the couch. Tears jumped to my eyes. My wife gathered up our son and took him to bed. But I did not stop telling anecdotes, which were coming in a rush. I recited them out loud, to myself. An American official—a new man, I didn't know him—appeared on screen and gave an account in a gruff voice. He looked frightened, listening to explosions in the distance.

I waited for my friend the diplomat. I had come to depend on him. But he was not interviewed that evening, nor was Nicholson anywhere in sight. Nick had probably gone up-country. The news shifted to Washington, a correspondent standing in the great circular driveway; in the background, figures moved on the porch of the mansion. Of course, it was dusk in Washington. The correspondent had information from confidential sources, none of whom were prepared to appear on camera or permit the use of their names. But the situation in the Zone was . . . very grave, desperate, in fact, and they in the White House seemed courageously prepared for the inevitable. The reliable sources described the atmosphere as tense but calm. The correspondent leaned into the camera, I knew him as a bon vivant; now he was selling gravity as he would sell soap or automobiles. He despised his métier, but the camera was kind to him.

The news ended and another program replaced it. I refilled my glass but did not move to turn off the set. I had arranged a drinks tray, so everything was within easy reach. I watched a game show, noisy with hysterical contestants and a frantic master of ceremonies. My time in the Zone came back to me in bits and pieces—an exotic tapestry. It was with me part of every day in any event, but now, concentrating, I discovered forgotten material. The patterns changed according to the distance you were from it, one of Escher's devilish constructions. It was like reading a well-loved novel years later and finding fresh turns of plot and character to admire. I remembered a friend saying once that if you were lucky enough to discover Trollope in middle age you'd never do without, because you could never live long enough to read all he wrote. I felt that way about the war, so remarkably dense an experience, with such treasure still buried. My Trollope war, so rich with incident and the friendships were forever. The diplomat and I had had many escapades.

Upstairs, I heard my wife reading to our son.

Come on down! I shouted.

The door opened. What do you want? My wife asked.

I want to tell you about the war! On television, the master of ceremonies gestured grandly at the balcony and yelled, Come on down!

She said something I didn't hear and closed the door.

I didn't notice. I was too drunk to notice. I had been

drunk for a month, since well before the final offensive of the People's Army and the collapse of the Free World Forces. So the offensive was not a cause of my drinking, or an excuse or justification for it. But it was not a reason to stop, either.

◊

The year 1975 was turbulent and even now I have difficulty sorting it out. Public affairs seemed to loom over us, darkening the prospect. Of course Nixon was already gone. Ford was soon to go. Each day brought weird revelations. The attorney general went to jail. The disgraced vice-president was frequently photographed at Las Vegas and was said to be making a killing as a corporate consultant, import-export. There was a picture in the newspaper of him shaking hands with Joe Louis, his fingers on the Brown Bomber's shoulder as if they were friends. The vice-president's tan was so deep, he could have been the champion's brother; he was smiling, obviously enjoying himself in Vegas. Joe wore a plastic golf cap, looking old and ruined. I went on the wagon for a month.

There were changes in the north country as well. A Venezuelan bought the dairy farm down the road from my house, the purchase conducted through nominees. An article in a business paper asserted that for the rich in nations of social and political unrest, New England farmland was as desirable as Krugerrands or Old Masters. The Venezuelan was followed by an industrialist from Peru, who bought a horse farm. The columnist in the local paper complained that the lingua franca in the valley would soon be Spanish. He took to describing our selectmen as "the junta" and predicting revolution. Then he announced that he himself was emigrating to Maine, at least the Abnaki spoke English and were indisputably North American. My wife and I briefly discussed putting our house on the market, then thought better of it; we were in the north country to stay, she said. There were other confusing portents. A large New York bank failed and nearly brought down the valley bank with it. The chairman explained at a party one night that his bank had gone heavily into Eurodollars on the expert advice of the president of the New York bank, a close personal friend who owned a condominium in the ski area nearby. The president facilitated these purchases, one banker lending his expertise to another. That was the reason there was no mortgage money in the valley: it was all in Europe and disappearing fast.

The news from Indochina after the fall of Saigon was fragmentary, and weeks would pass with no reports on the evening news. No news was not good news. I thought of it as a dark and threatening silence, as unpropitious in its way as the deep restless fastness of the woods surrounding my house. When, later, the Chinese invaded north Vietnam the dominoes trembled, but held; so fathead Dulles had been at once right and wrong about the course of events in Southeast Asia.

I was writing a history of the war. I completed the book in good time, all but the final chapter. For my description of the end of the war I was obliged to depend on the recollections of others. I decided to write a simple reconstruction of the final battle. Six times I went to Washington to interview civilians from the State Department and CIA and the Pentagon, and military officers everywhere in the city. Many were friends from the previous decade and were generous with their time; we knew many of the same stories. I obtained classified documents, but these did not clarify the situation; they were secret but not very interesting, and often false or misleading. Facts piled up, but I could not fit them together in any plausible way. What had seemed so clear in front of the television set now seemed erratic and unfocused, drunken events reeling from day to day with no logic or plan. And what was the consequence, other than the obvious thing? I was unable to interview my friend the diplomat, who had been posted to another, very remote embassy; there was a rumor he was on the outs with the

Department. We corresponded for a time but his letters were perfunctory, and he declined to volunteer any fresh facts or fresh interpretations of the known facts. I was disappointed but not surprised. He had always been a very discreet official.

I knew that a simple reconstruction of the final battle was not enough. Through friends who had been active in the antiwar movement I applied for a visa to Vietnam, but was put off; perhaps later, when the situation stabilized. No one was getting in then.

I told my wife, I can't end this book.

You have got to let it go, she said.

The *book*? I asked incredulously. She couldn't know what she was asking.

The war, she said furiously.

◇

I went on writing. I did not watch television much, though many of the faces in the new administration were familiar. They were experienced men, chosen by the President to inspire confidence, having served in administrations from the previous decade. Everyone agreed, there was no substitute for experience at the highest levels of government, even during dark times. However, the President believed there was a crisis of the American spirit. There was narcissism and malaise, and the American people had to put these dark times behind them in order to advance to greatness. Narcissism and materialism threatened progress; the people had become pessimistic, they were so preoccupied by the past. The people had to be tough of mind and spirit; they had to *forget*.

My last chapter wouldn't come.

One afternoon, disgusted by the day's yield, I left my desk and went outside. Although the temperature was near zero, I was in my shirtsleeves. Standing on my unprotected deck, I looked west at the mountains, which on bright days bounded the valley in various shades of blue. My wife maintained that at dusk there were seven different shades of blue that changed as you watched them, like a musical piece changing key. There were no houses visible, or any sign of civilization. It could have been a wilderness anywhere, these deserted and silent highlands. We had had a thaw, then a sharp freeze. The ground was hard as iron, the dead leaves brittle underfoot. I stood motionless in the cold, listening. I did not flinch when I heard the familiar sound, though it gave rise to a crawling fear. It came from the west and I searched the sky, trying to stand at ease, inconspicuous on my own property; but my feet would not obey and I danced away into the corner, under the eaves. At last I located it, low and approaching from the tree line, a moving object in the dull blue, and growing. No one who has ever heard the sound in wartime will ever forget, slap*slap*slap*slap*. I watched him approach over my empty quarter, dipping a little, then rising, flying contour only a few feet above my firs and bare maples. Very close now, the nose suddenly dipped and the Huey turned like a runner reversing field, skidding, its engine screaming, and banked dizzyingly away, rising higher in circles and flying off to the south. I watched it go, seeing the pink excited face in the passenger seat, a quick grin, and a too-casual salute—my banker friend, Eurodollar Ed, scouting the valley for a developer.

I was trembling with fear and memory; the Zone had been singular in its urgency and restless vitality. I had been so long in this place, I could not see the future; the past blocked my vision. I was alone with my cocktails, my interviews, my boy, and my increasingly aggrieved wife. Now it was another late fall, with infinite winter in the sullen air, the winter that went on forever. As the sound of the chopper faded and then ceased altogether, I understood that I had been living inside my history of the war, my feverish memory of it; this year was that year relived, but in a cold and lonely climate.

I shivered suddenly, hearing a car door slam and my wife's voice, high and insistent. She and the boy were back from the market. I stepped off the deck and walked to the edge of the woods. It was so cold. I heard her call but I did not answer. I felt a sharp sting on my face and remembered that snow had been forecast. It would be heavy, the first of the season. Various country portents indicated a hard winter. The prospects were excellent for snow all night long, and for the season. My wife called again and I moved farther into the woods, away from her voice. This place was so remote, perhaps that was what she meant by returning to the fundamentals. Snow fell heavier now, and from my redoubt in the woods I watched my son skylark on the deck. He was a sturdy boy, built like a fireplug, brimming with energy, always cheerful. Shivering still, I longed for the damp heat of Asia and the thick sweat that came after a long walk in the hot sun. I advanced into the woods, until the house was no longer visible. My son called twice, then gave up and went inside. I heard the door bang twice. I continued to walk into the woods, whitening now, the snow striking and melting on my face and bare arms. I came to a clearing and paused under a big maple. I thought of myself as a swimmer striking out to sea: this terrain was as monotonous as any ocean. Then I smelled the syrupy sweet smoke from our wood stove, and that reminded me of the sour charcoal smell of Asian villages.

I remembered accompanying a patrol once, it was a routine sweep in the Delta somewhere. My friend the diplomat had asked to go along; he was then a junior man, new to the embassy, and had never been on a military operation. It was strictly against the rules, but he was determined to do it. We left the Caravelle early in the morning and by noon we were slogging through rice fields with an incompetent ARVN platoon. We walked and walked, and it was too hot to talk so I was silent. At length, bothered by my silence, he asked me if anything was wrong. What was I thinking about? I said I was so bored I was planning my funeral. He thought that very funny and laughed all the way back to base. Just the other day he sent me a letter recalling the incident and what I had said. I had forgotten completely about it and laughed as I read the letter. My wife looked up and asked me what was so funny. I deliberated a moment, then passed it off without comment. She would not have understood. How could I explain that on a personal level the experience of the war was inalienable. You could not share it or transfer it or communicate it in any recognizable form. It was yours alone, your own shadow, a doppelgänger present night and day.

She thought, reasonably, that I was driving her away. My moods, my drinking, my pessimism, my excess, my nightmares, my zeal, my boredom; my memory had become a penitentiary. I refused to accommodate myself to the north country, being so preoccupied by the war and by Asia. She said I reminded her of her father, so often absent on business; he was a great traveler when she was a girl, and even when he was present he was somehow absent. Just like you, she said. Her father had been in the war, five years in the Pacific Theater; and he never spoke of it at all. Of course he had not been an important journalist, a prizewinner. He had been a colonel of intelligence, and when he returned to his family it was as if he had never been away. Later, he was often gone on business. Even now she could hear the slam of the front door and his voice, always the same, the same words: Hello! Hello inside! I'm back! The Boss is home! And everyone rushing to greet him—her mother, her younger sister, her older brother—as if he were Marco Polo.

So perhaps that was what war did to men, gave them an itch, made them restless and discontented; though with me it was more than itch and restlessness. My discontent was like a sickness threatening to overwhelm us all. She shrewdly declared that I was like the man who had constructed a ship in a bottle, stick by wee stick. To release the ship I would have to break the bottle, and that I was unwilling to do—was afraid of doing—but until I did I would have no rest, nor would she.

It's a no-win situation, she said.

For whom? I asked.

◇

We talked it over one morning at the kitchen table. The breakfast dishes had been cleared away and we sat at the bare table in the glum half-light of midmorning. I toyed with the saltcellar and looked into her dark eyes, then over her shoulder through the silders into the gray valley, the heavy clouds above, and the range rising beyond. She was wearing old corduroys and a blue wool shirt, and her hair was back in a ponytail, tied with a silk scarf; she loved the rough masculine clothes of the north country, though she always managed to add a feminine, sexy touch. We had sat across the table from each other so many times, it was where we habitually discussed family business; it was a refectory table and six feet separated us. Her voice was low and husky. I was just fooling myself, she said. She continued, I have been an idiot not to have seen it before now. But you have to go away somewhere, it's obvious. You have to get your head together, go away for a while, forget about things; and when you come back, make sure they stay forgotten. She said, I'm sick and tired of living in a haunted house. We were silent a moment. I spilled some salt and threw it over my left shoulder, for luck. Then she said, Go visit one of your friends. She named several who lived in Washington and one who lived in New York. Why not one of them? The hunting season's open, isn't it? My friend the diplomat owned a place on the Eastern Shore, a pretty farm on the Wye with two duck blinds in the backyard. Go there, she said. Go kill ducks. But he was abroad on assignment and the house was rented. I explained that, and also that I did not want to go to Washington.

Washington's regressive, I said, intending to make a joke.

But she did not smile. She said at last, Then go see

Quinn. That's what you want to do, anyway, I can tell. And it'll be quite a meeting of minds, I wouldn't mind being a fly on the wall. He's just as irresponsible as you are.

I smiled. She was right on the first point, wrong on the second. Quinn was not irresponsible. He had no responsibilities, how could he be irresponsible? We had argued the point many times and agreed to disagree. My friend Quinn was never less than controversial. I put water on for coffee.

This isn't getting us anywhere, she said.

I stood watching the kettle, waiting for it to boil. I wanted to get away, no question of that, and controversial Quinn was convenient. Visiting Quinn was like visiting an exotic foreign land. There was so much to see and do! We both lit cigarettes, the smoke hanging heavily in the dim, silent room. The flame under the kettle was the only artificial light, a dull blue. Presently the water began to hiss.

A change of scene, she said wearily.

I nodded. That would be Quinn all right.

She said, My father had a friend like Quinn.

Family patterns, I thought. Women were obsessed by them. To a woman, there was nothing new under the sun.

She said, He lived in Boston and, when my father went to Boston on business, that's where he stayed. They had been in school together, I think, and at one time he had dated my mother. He was so mysterious, I never met him until my father's funeral. He wore a Borsalino and a mustache, very dapper. I met him then and have never seen him since. My mother told me later that he never married but had a mistress. I don't know if the mistress was a live-in mistress or not.

I said, She wasn't.

My wife looked at me, surprised. How do you know?

Your father told me, I said.

When? When did he tell you?

I don't know, I said. One night, we were talking. He told me about Charles, the life he led and the fun they had.

20

It was innocent enough, a few too many drinks in the Ritz bar and then dinner at Locke's. Sometimes they'd end up in the mistress's apartment for a cognac. Your father was always amused by the mistress, who was no cupcake. But she was humorous and full of life. She wouldn't marry Charles because she had a huge alimony from her first husband and the alimony'd stop the minute she remarried and while Charles had some money he didn't have as much as her first husband and she'd gotten used to a certain style of life and didn't intend to give it up not even for Charles, she said.

My wife said, I wonder where she is now.

I shrugged, I didn't know.

And Charles. I wonder where he is.

I didn't know that, either. I said, Probably wherever she is.

Christ, she said. She lit another cigarette.

I looked up from the kettle, whistling now. I said, You're smoking too much.

She said, How would you like to kiss my ass? She was so angry. She banged her fists on the table. My restlessness and unease had always been a thing between us, worse in their way than the war—or were they the same thing? What did I want from her?

She said to me, We came to the north country to get back to fundamentals—

Yes, I replied. That was the trouble.

two

We were both correct and of course there could be no compromise; we were fighting for our lives. In any hand-to-hand combat the vital rule is to move in close, attacking, a risky strategy but the one that holds a promise of victory. But I had so many enemies and I could not sort them out. I was outnumbered, at war with the north country itself and everyone in it, and unquestionably with the "fundamentals" as well—whatever they were, they were by no means as clear to me as they were to my wife, or as benevolent. The forested north country, with its extremes of temperature, terrain, and psychology, was no place to mediate or bargain. There were no honest brokers, and its austerity discouraged magnanimity, in the way a dour or unfriendly audience chills a performer. Yet its extremes were beguiling; the courageous thing was not to run from it but to close with it, persevere in an advance to its very heart. In the end you were always your own broker.

So I made preparations to evacuate—a temporary measure, I told myself. I needed time off, some rest & recreation at Quinn's playground in the Northeast Kingdom. The moment I made this decision (how prescient my wife had been, how helpful, her light cut through the darkness), I felt a tranquillity and certainty I had not felt since the exhilarating commencement of the war. I was in control again, on assignment. In my exhilaration, I knew my whole life had been leading to this point. I was in the middle distance, poised to observe the previous decade and from its contours weigh the present and forecast the future. I knew my decision was a self-seeking act, and a kind of psychosis; it was very much in the spirit of the age. That was obvious. But as everyone knows, something altogether special can be created in psychosis. I took psychosis to mean extreme animation, a kind of delirious or lunatic holiday on credit. No foreboding: it would be an extraordinary and cheerful adventure with no immediate accounting or predictable consequence.

◇

I took inventory that morning, three hours' worth. There was the manuscript—more than six hundred pages—and the notebooks. There were fifty of them, mostly interviews, each notebook identified with a name, a date, and a place. Handling them, I felt a particular kinship. One wall of my study was covered with photographs in black frames, infantrymen on patrol or in trouble. I looked at them often to remind me of the damp heat and of the stunned look of fear, of the various shapes of the gear, weapons, packs, helmets, fatigues, and of the machines, helicopter gunships, tanks, APCs, Jeeps, and the four-wheel-drive Scouts the civilians used. The photographs jogged my memory no less than the notebooks; there was a story behind each one. On the wall over my filing cabinet were the dago dazzlers, as Quinn called them: my Pulitzer and the two OPC awards and the others, and a letter from the secretary of defense denouncing me to my publisher. There were no family photographs, except one of my wife and son together, tucked into the bookshelf next to Giap, Guevara, and Grivas.

I wanted the manuscript with me, so I packed it and the notebooks into a duffel. My desk looked naked without the thick stack of paper, weighted with a Buddha's head.

As an afterthought, I threw the Buddha into the duffel, too. I took a last look at the photographs and straightened my desk. I covered my typewriter and put the thesaurus, dictionary, and almanac away. The house was silent except for the hiss of the wood-burning stove. My wife and son were out shopping and would be gone all day long. We had made our good-byes after breakfast, my son cranky because I wouldn't take him with me. Outside, the duffel in one hand and my suitcase in the other, I paused and listened. Somewhere nearby a chainsaw growled, a sound as familiar and constant as auto horns in mid-Manhattan. I put the duffel and the suitcase in the trunk of the car. I drove down the old road, and was away.

Have a good time, she'd said. We had partially made up, to the point where there was truce, or anyway cease-fire. She and the boy were at the door, anxious to be off. The smell of bacon and coffee was all around us.

I never get to do anything, he said.

I said, It'll only be a few days. A week at the most.

Yes, she said. Whatever. We'll be here. You'll definitely be at Quinn's, then?

Yes, I said, and gave her the telephone number. She looked at it and put the piece of paper on the bulletin board. Quinn's number was unlisted, unless you knew the code. He listed himself under the name of his alter ego, Tom Plumb. Not that anyone could remember the name of the town he lived near. It was very far north.

You always get to do everything, the boy said.

Tell him hello, my wife said.

Let's go, he said.

I said, Maybe we'll get some skiing in. It looks like snow.

Yes, she said. Then she smiled. I'd like to see that, you on the slopes. Watch you don't break your hip. Anyway, there isn't any Ritz bar or Locke's.

No, I said. No chance of that.

Is he alone? she asked.

Quinn's never alone, I said.

That's right, she said brightly. Of course that's right, how stupid of me. And now he'll have you, too.

I remembered all of that, each word, as I drove down the old road and turned north, away from our town and its atmosphere of civilized rustication. It had changed so in the years we'd lived there. In 1973 it had been a pretty little dying village, the half a dozen resident artists and writers guarding its anonymity with the zeal of gourmets guarding the location of a fine, inexpensive restaurant. The ski area changed that, and now there were articles in the travel sections of newspapers. Television crews from Boston and New York prowled Main Street looking for local color. Everyone agreed, Eurodollar Ed had done a hell of a job: condominium money was coming into the valley, and prosperity was just around the corner. We ridiculed it—but we were fascinated, too; I came to think of the valley as a colony, like the Costa Brava or Nassau, its economy controlled by absentee landlords.

Our town was at the edge of the picturesque mountainous zone. Twenty miles north the land flattens and the forests thin, nature's entropy. The mountains peter out to mere hills, and even the trees are shorter and scrawnier. Panoramas vanish and what beauty there is is in miniature. This region is not quaint, only poor; as the natives say, It is close to God and Canada. But it supports life, and as the natives also say, Never criticize the bridge that carries you safely across. Two-hundred-year-old towns nestle close to small seedy rivers; here and there are red-brick mills, sturdy as fortresses, vacant now. The mills always seemed to be located at a pretty part of the river, a bend or a rapids; the marriage of aesthetics and convenience. They manufactured essentials: shoes, bobbins, woolens, lumber. All that was gone, and had been gone for many years. The towns crouch, huddled against the weather, never more than a few stores and a gas station, and no traffic lights to delay the busy motorist or trucker. The few people on the sidewalks are aged but hearty. Things move slowly, to a different time. It is hard to know what occupies people here, and where the money comes from. There is little industry and no tourism, except for the occasional deer hunter or trout fisherman, come to set up camp near the Nulhegan or the Clyde or the two beautiful lakes, Willoughby and Memphremagog. But they aren't big spenders. Still, the large white houses, with their rambling porches, sharp gables, and belvederes, sport discreet signs:

ROOMS
INQUIRE WITHIN

earning a few extra dollars a season to supplement savings and the Social Security. North of our town there were no boutiques or piano bars, and no young people, either; this was not the end of the line but its beginning. I thought of it as North America in 1955 or before, except that the inhabitants were old and the towns worn out. It was Eisenhower's America—the churches so pretty, white, and modest, and congenial to the surroundings. I guessed that the prayers were modest, too. I often drove here to get away from the isolation of my place or from the youth and complexity of our town in the valley—from the chaste to the ultrachaste. This far north, there was very little news of urgency or consequence; it was a landlocked region and the important news was private. It was always a nice drive, and I had cause to observe that the real beauty of it was man-made, a barn and its silo, a rail fence, a child's swing hanging from the thick branch of a sugar maple, or an old party bending to peer into a mailbox at the end of a driveway.

I drove slowly, in no hurry, as I knew the route well. Nothing ever changed along it so there was nothing to interfere with my reverie, which had cheered and amused me since the moment I left home. Driving over the mountain, my way out, I began to place writers I'd loved and grown distant from during my time in the country. I conceived of my homeland as a great clinic, the American Hospital: Dr.

Twain, chief of surgery, he supervised a number of distinguished associates; Dr. Dreiser, the bone man; Dr. Eliot, chaplain; Drs. Stevens and Jarrell, internists; Dr. Faulkner, chief pathologist; Dr. Hemingway, director of the trauma unit; and Dr. Fitzgerald, general practitioner. Dr. Lowry, our British cousin, was loitering somewhere near the operating room, *perfectamente borracho*. And on the ground floor, in a huge consulting room all to himself, dwelled Dr. James, chief of psychiatry. I had grown very distant from James in my return to the fundamentals in remote New England. His paragraphs were as dense as the woods and his sentences as tortuous as the switchback trail to the summit of the mountain due west of my house. We had lost touch, Dr. James and I. In the past I'd read all his books for inspiration and consolation at those times when, following impulse, I'd run the scale, changing tempos, harmonies, all the rules of music. . . . *strike as many notes, deep, full and rapid, as one can*. . . . Do as I say, not as I do. James in the jungle, the spoils of James. I consumed the canon, but each time the Master was a little less consoling. I reckoned he did not have much personal experience with running the scale and with disharmony, or with the casualties that result from improvisation. A great field marshal, he was aware of the smallest details, yet never lost sight of the objective. I saw him as Bonaparte on the hilltop at Borodino, wheeling armies into battle. Bonaparte with his nine-o'clock-in-the-morning courage. From his summit he heard the explosions and witnessed the clamor of battle, its noise and confusion and restless movement, its terror and awful randomness—but remote, too, a field of smoke and miniature men advancing into a many-colored maw. Field marshals never heard the screams or dried the blood; and the tears, if any, were their own and the result not of pain but of anguish. They were not obliged to attend to private soldiers, except to hand out the medals in the surgery later. James's exhortation was attractive if you were James. It didn't make it less true or less poignant or noble or attractive if you were not James, only less authoritative.

I turned right off the macadam road, driving very slowly now. The woods began to thicken again, and here and there great maples stood out among the firs. The forest looked somehow tended, as if there were a hired man to care for it. I smiled: a can of Heineken rested on a stump beside the road. Quinn's welcome. I stopped the car, got out, and stood listening to the silence. A faint odor of wood smoke was in the air. I hopped the ditch and touched the can with my fingertips. It was still cold, so I cracked it and drank. I stood with one foot on the stump, rocking back and forth, drinking the cold beer. No inventory of literary men would be complete without an accounting of Quinn, new man in the burn ward, his modern specialty plastic surgery. Quinn, my oldest friend, whose door was always ajar. Quinn, who craved society as I craved solitude. Nine months a year he lived stylishly in London, off Chester Square in a maisonette the color of vichyssoise. October, November, and December he hibernated, more or less, in the Northeast Kingdom, writing. His house had been built by a lumber baron as a summer retreat, and sold because the lumber baron's wife hated the loneliness and severity of the wilderness. She preferred Provincetown; in Provincetown there was gaiety, and no bears to ravage her pygmy roses and no raccoons to scavenge the garbage. The house itself was a wandering affair of clapboard and fieldstone, a structure more suited to Sharon or Gloucester than to the north country; it had cost a fortune to build and was not cheap to maintain. There was a tennis court in back, but the net was always down and mushrooms had pushed through the Har-Tru. The garden with the pygmy roses had been let go. Except for a small lawn in front, the wilderness had reclaimed the land; and it was not a benign wilderness. Quinn said he preferred it that way, the terrain in its natural state. The house had been on the market for two years when Quinn bought it. That was five years ago, and now he referred to it as "my American office."

I finished the Heineken and got back in my car. I had been playing a tape of the Benny Goodman 1938 Carnegie Hall Jazz Concert. I turned the volume up and sat for a moment, thinking about Quinn, author of a dozen mystery novels, all of which featured a newspaperman. Each year he produced a new novel, finishing it in his American office in the fall and early winter, always writing the final sentence the day after Christmas; he was as disciplined as Trollope. The stories invariably took place in a cold climate, somewhere north of the fifty-fifth parallel, and in a political milieu. Quinn was a connoisseur of parliamentary atmosphere, where casual conversation was as deadly as a knife fight. They were sexy stories, Quinn maintained, because the newspaperman always fell in love with a suspect, usually the guilty party. When the case was concluded, he went back to his wife, no happier but no wiser, either. Like Ian Fleming, who created James Bond at the precise moment when secret agents replaced army generals as heroes of the cold war, Quinn created Tom Plumb at the height of the Indochina war, when newspapermen replaced novelists as the most reliable interpreters of public reality and menace. With the advent of Watergate, the success of the series was assured. Tom Plumb became as well known as Nero Wolfe or George Smiley, and Quinn became a millionaire.

I dickered with the tape deck until I found Jess Stacy's solo in "Sing Sing Sing"—dah dah *dah*, dah dah dahdah *dah*—and Goodman's appreciative "yes, yes" as he pulled the microphone closer to the piano. Then I lowered the window, turned the volume on full, and accelerated up the road. Quinn's house was around the next bend behind a low stone wall. When I pulled into the drive he was waiting on the tiny lawn, huge in greatcoat, muffler, and deerstalker. He did a little boogie to the music and we embraced with shouts and laughter, our breath pluming in the chilly air.

He said, "You didn't bring her."

I laughed. "No."

He rolled his eyes. "Good thing, comrade. It's no time

for quarrels. And I've got you a date, marvelous creature, better than you deserve. Thank God, she doesn't break easily. You'll love her, she's out of the ordinary and a little off the wall." He peered at me closely. "Where is she?" Quinn couldn't bring himself to pronounce my wife's name. They were not well met—a matter of personal metabolism; in fact, they had not spoken in two years. It was one reason why Quinn and I did not see each other often.

I said, "Home."

"A woman's place," he said, rolling his eyes again.

"No," I said. "But that's where she is, or's supposed to be."

"Christ," he said. "It's cold." We went inside. I dropped my bags in the hall and followed him into the study. He had a bottle of champagne in a bucket and immediately poured two glasses. While Quinn busied himself with hors d'oeuvres, I looked around the familiar study. I had not been to this house in a year, but it looked unchanged. There were a number of photographs of Quinn and me with various notables—Harold Macmillan at a garden party at a country house in Kent a few years ago, Georg Brunis at a jazz club in Chicago in the late fifties, Edith Piaf on a beach in the south of France. That was 1962, the year before Piaf died, though she looked dead then; Quinn had had a letter of introduction from an American impresario, and Piaf seemed amused at meeting two young American men. There was one of Quinn in soup-and-fish at a dinner in the Guildhall, and one of me at a microphone at the 1968 Democratic National Convention, where I had been a radio commentator, familiar with both Chicago and the war. A year later I took an editor's job and four years after that was out of the business altogether, though you never completely left journalism: too many memories.

He had arranged pâté and a Stilton and pumpernickel bread on two plates and set them on the coffee table. "What's happened to the book?"

"Stalled," I said.

"I suppose you can't end it."

Quinn had an instinct for the jugular. I nodded.

He smiled. "I'm almost finished with mine."

"Swell," I said.

He said, "Plumb in Love."

I said it was a good title. He was always very good at entitling his books.

"But before we get down to the hard tack," he said, "we must have pleasure." There was a party that evening. People were arriving from all over the region. Quinn was expansive, listing the guests by name, occupation, and personal eccentricity. I listened attentively, though I knew most of them. I admired their spirit, commuting to Quinn's house at the back of beyond, though it was true that his parties were famous. There was one surprise, a retired diplomat and his wife and their houseguests. I knew the houseguests; he was labor attaché at the embassy in Brussels and his wife ran a small wine business. They were on home leave.

Improbably, everyone lived within a fifty-mile radius of Quinn's house, and fifty miles was nothing in the north country. Also, Quinn said shyly, there was his new girl friend, Tessa Dane. Surely I had heard of the New York Danes—rich, very rich and notorious—Tessa's brutish father was the luminous Jack "Great" Dane, no stranger to the pages of *Fortune* and *Sports Illustrated*. He owned horse-flesh and mines. Her mother was the infamous Betsy, one-time darling of the OSS, woman-about-town, and matchless raconteur. "My life has taken an erratic turn," he said. He looked up at me and laughed, prodding me with his glass: more drink. "I'm glad as hell you got out of there, comrade. On the phone it sounded bad, very bad, and only likely to get worse."

"Was," I said. "Is." I didn't want to talk about it then.

"This girl," he began, "the marvelous creature we've gotten for you. Her name is Marty Neher."

"I might stay awhile," I said.

He shrugged, I could stay as long as I wanted.

"Maybe through Christmas," I said.

Quinn shrugged again. So what? One week, two; a month, two months. It was all one to him, so long as I was quiet in the mornings when he was working. He began an involved anecdote about the girl, she and Tessa had become good friends. . . .

I was looking out the window, at the teeth of a rock outcropping and the woods beyond. Dusk was coming on and there was drizzle. Quinn rose to stoke the fire and in a moment it caught and leapt, blazing. The woods began to disappear in the dusk and drizzle. Of course there were no lights anywhere outside. I listened to Quinn talk about the girl, who she was and where she came from. Tonight or tomorrow night my wife and son would cut a small tree for Christmas. There was one particular spruce, deep in the woods in a stand of maple, that was nice-sized and shapely. It would be a job getting it back to the house, though. I said, "Tell me about Tessa."

"She came with me from London. She's been here all this time and's gotten on pretty well, considering that this place is not exactly Chester Square. Harrod's and the Antelope are not around the corner, no." He poured champagne for us both. "Our first meeting, it was wonderful, not to be improved upon. It was like the opening chapter of one of my books!"

"Aren't they all?" I said.

"Everything's material," he said grimly, and began to tell the story. Listening to Quinn, I forgot about my wife and son and whatever difficulty there would be in getting the spruce through the woods to the house. In this study, with its brown leather chairs and bookshelves and photographs of famous men and women in silver frames, its Perrier-Jouet in a bucket and gnarled Stilton on a bone-white plate, the north country was far away. It was typical that there was no view from Quinn's house. Quinn said that if he had wanted a view he would have moved to Cornwall or Northumberland. On still evenings you could stand on the porch and hear water running in a stream, almost inaccessible through the forest. Indisputably an American, he lived here as Englishmen had lived in the remote colonies—northern India, perhaps, or Rhodesia before the unpleasantness.

He loved noise and speed, confusion and hustle. His life was so different from mine—stepping into it was like stepping through the looking glass of a novel, the ambience as dense and particular as anything in Dickens or Waugh. Quinn led a teeming melodrama of a life, rich with people and things and never less than controversial. It always took me a day or two to catch up with him when we met; we ran different races to different clocks. Quinn seemed to hurtle through the years with no backward glances, and whatever second thoughts he had he kept to himself. No remorse, no regrets. Of course he had his books and his books had their dark side. I listened to him tell his story, my own memory nagging at me.

◇

They'd met at a party in Regent's Park. Quinn's name meant nothing to her and she held to the English habit of never asking people what they did for a living. This did not deter Quinn, who explained in detail. He gave her a florid character sketch of his newspaperman, Tom Plumb. Aggressive romantic, heterosexual.

"My name is Quinn, not Queen."

He supplied the numbers, so many books in print on the various continents and in the Low Countries. While he spoke of his royalties he grinned and eyed her suspiciously, stroking his beard. Quinn was large and florid, a rumpled bear with thinning brown hair and gray Hemingway whiskers. The whiskers either advanced his age or reduced it, depending on his condition and the time of day.

"Is this true?" he asked. "You never heard of me?"

"I never read detectives," she said.

"Hell of a thing," he said, looking hurt.

33

"It doesn't mean anything."

"Well," he said, "a man spends fifteen years of his life writing *books*—"

She said, "You're raising your voice."

"—translated in six languages, meets an attractive woman, never heard of him. Doesn't know him from damn-all. Hurts." He thumped his enormous chest. "Here." People were beginning to turn and look at them.

She began to laugh, this was egomania on a grand scale. She enjoyed him, most of the men she knew were modest. She said, "You've never heard of me, why should I've heard of you?"

"Heard of you," he said morosely.

"Balls," she said, knowing it was probably true. Quinn gave the impression of knowing everyone in the world. "You don't know my last name, what I do." She stared him down, still amused, then glanced over his shoulder at the other guests, tall men, pale women. Quinn's vitality was magnetic; they were being watched. Conversations elsewhere were conducted in a low murmur.

He was silent at last, evidently considering his next move. Then, suddenly: "Tessa Dane, painter of landscapes, promising artist. Though God knows what it is you're promising. You make promises to your public? I never do. I know your mother."

She was silent a moment, watching him.

Quinn continued, "You could be her younger sister." His voice was booming now, like the master of a quarter-deck. "Same eyes, same haircut, same reserve." He stepped back, appraising her. She had beautiful, clear skin, gray eyes, and a wide, sardonic mouth; he was bothered by her nose, a touch too large for the rest of her. He said, "You're pretty enough, you're damn pretty girl. Close my eyes and it could be her talking, same baritone, same snooty accent." He smiled brightly. "Thing is, are you as loony as she is?" He poured large drinks for them both, reaching over the

34

long table, ignoring the bartender. He brandished his glass, again eyeing her suspiciously.

She said, "I'm not loony."

"That's too bad."

"You think Mum's loony?"

He said, "Sure. Don't you?"

"I would've said zany."

"Whatever." He sighed and took a long swallow of his drink, looking across the room at their hostess. "Haven't seen your mum in a while, hoped she might be here. 'Stead, you are."

"Where'd you meet her?" she asked in a doubtful voice.

"Here."

"Well, I assumed. But where?"

"I mean *here*," he said impatiently, gesturing. "This house. Fact, same place we're standing. Same time of night, same second-rate bourbon, same slow-motion bartender. Same sad faces." He pulled a long face and she smiled; it was the truth, her mother drank bourbon. "We saw quite a lot of each other awhile ago." He stared at her and shook his head. "That nose you've got, that's not hers. I suppose that's one of Great's legacies. Hell of a legacy. Put you in knee britches and you're a Florentine prince."

She said, "What are you doing here?"

"Our hostess likes me. Thinks I'm a rough diamond. Thinks I write westerns. I'm the token American at this bash, was then, too. Your mum was the token loony."

Tessa said, "I wish you wouldn't call her that. I don't like it. And what do you mean, 'quite a lot'?"

"Oh," he said vaguely, "this and that. Here and there." Then he changed the subject. He asked her about her work, what it meant to her. To her surprise, she found herself answering his questions, which were shrewd and pertinent; he had a serious knowledge of painting. And when he asked her about Betsy and Great she found herself answering those questions, too. Her parents had been divorced for twenty years; her mother lived in London and her father in America. The fortune came from her father's great-grandfather. Quinn said, "Let me guess. They called him great-Great. Or would it be great-great Great." He was hugely amused by all this. He loved talking about money, whence it came, whither it went. He said, "Your old man must've given you advice. People like that are always free with advice. Own up. What was it? Advice to carry you through a mild recession."

She waited a moment before replying. She was in deeper than she wanted to be, though it was obvious that her mother must have told him a good deal. She asked him for a cigarette and he gave her one. Then she told him that her father warned her never to forget who she was, at those times she was tempted to be someone else. "He said, 'It won't work. You are who you are. This family is like a very old cognac. That's what it is. It isn't any other kind of spirits and it isn't improved by the addition of ice or soda water. If you do add ice or soda water, the cognac's still there, only understrength. And remember, I control your trust fund.' " She blew a smoke ring at him, grinning. "My father is not a likable man."

They went to a restaurant in Mayfair. He was never silent and they both drank too much. Tessa decided he was enchanting in his weird and blustering way, filled with strange information, an American who knew about *things* and was not reluctant to share his knowledge. He knew how to repair a television set, understood the politics of the Vatican, could recite Balzac from memory. "I learned French from *Père Goriot*, text in one hand, trot in the other." They closed the restaurant at midnight, then went to his house in Chester Square.

Belgravia, in its hush and Georgian equilibrium, was an odd location for an American of Quinn's temperament. They stood in the street while he described its provenance; he had researched his predecessors at Number 190 and had discovered a brigadier, a banker, a Welsh baronet, and a whore. He was convinced that MI-6 had owned the house during the war, a safe house, he said, for the use of fleeing Polish émigrés. Where this information came from, he refused to divulge. Inside, one anticipated Persian carpets, Chippendale cabinets, Constables, and a servant. One found instead a lurid neon sculpture, an Art Deco wet bar, a lime tree, and a white piano. Hanging above the piano were two photographs, portraits of Quinn and a woman. Quinn was caught in profile, a cigarette drooping from his mouth, a corona of smoke over his head; his eyes were downcast, half closed against the smoke. Tessa stared at the other portrait, wondering who she was. It was not a very flattering portrait, but it was impossible to know whether that was the fault of the photographer or of the woman.

"It's a good one of you," Tessa said. "Who's she?"

Quinn said, "A woman I know."

Tessa moved back a step, she had heard an echo and knew exactly what that meant. She said, "Shit," exhaling.

"No," Quinn said. "She's not shit. She's very nice."

"I don't care if she's a shit or not a shit. That isn't what I meant. Where is she now?"

"America."

"Back tomorrow, I suppose."

"No," Quinn said shortly.

Tessa sat on the piano bench and looked at the portrait. She was a woman about Quinn's age, early forties. She was in repose, head tilted, listening, yet her gaze was direct, almost a challenge. Her hair was swept back in the American manner, and her shoulders were covered by a black shawl. She giggled, Whistler's mistress. A faint suggestion of contempt spoiled the mouth. That photographer was no friend, Tessa decided. Quinn's wife was probably more alluring in real life than in the portrait. Tessa sighed—an obvious sigh, an obvious mistake. And she had not picked up any of it. Quinn had in no way behaved like a married man, there were none of the little evasions and pauses that hint at another life. She looked at him without expression.

"I suppose the children are upstairs in bed. Of course there would be two children, Americans are so practical. Let me see. These children would be a boy and a girl, aged seven and nine. You will be careful to lock the bedroom door tonight in case Precious wants to roughhouse with Daddy in the morning. You will want me out of the house at first light so you can take them to the fucking zoo. Am I warm?"

Grinning, he leaned down and kissed her lightly. "Surprise, there are no children."

"Well, isn't that ducky. I suppose the children are in America with their mommy. They call each day with news of their adventures—"

"No. No children period."

"Even better. Are you impotent? Or selfish?"

"No," he said thoughtfully, imperturbable as stone. He moved away from her and stood under the portrait. "That's not the way it is. I am not married. I have never been married. And Carla and I have an arrangement."

Tessa said, "Aren't you just the little modern man, now? Isn't that just *super!* Christ, Quinn."

"Not modern," Quinn said.

"I've been through it before. It's so tiresome."

He nodded solemnly. "I can guess. Probably in his late thirties. Wife and children in the 'burbs somewhere. Wimbledon. Stock broker? Art dealer? There would've been a scene, very dramatic. One of Iris Murdoch's scenes. He probably told you it was all over just after the entrée, in a crowded restaurant. He'd pour the wine and not quite look you in the eye. 'She needs me. The children need me. Gulp. Sniffle.' "

"Close enough," she said. "And I promised myself it would never happen again, never ever. Made a res'lution and I never make res'lutions."

"Me either," he said. "Or scenes."

"Now you. You with your wife in America. Your 'arrangement.' "

"She's not my wife," Quinn said.

"Same difference," Tessa said.

"No, it's not."

"Who is she then?"

"Never mind who she is," Quinn said.

"The long-lost love?"

He said nothing for a moment. A woman's instinct was remorseless, and he would have to wait for it to tire; in time it would blow itself out, like a wind. He said, "You're here now and I'm too drunk to drive you home."

"I'm too drunk to go home," she said miserably.

"We had a good time tonight until you got stupid and I got sore." She nodded, that was true enough.

He began to talk in a low voice, a voice so soft it lulled her. It was something to do with Carla, a woman who was of his life but not in it—if she understood the difference. He moved her off the piano stool and to the couch, where she had a clear view of the portrait over the white piano. She waited for the approach, the arm around her neck, his cognac breath, and she was composing a retort, something devastating—perhaps she would begin to cry and when he crooned at her, comforting her, she would rise and announce, They weren't tears, you idiot, *I'm yawning*. . . . A man with an ego as big as Quinn's, it would kill him; just kill him.

But he left her and returned to the piano and began to play, very old, slow blues. He played wonderfully, his huge hands moving light as feathers across the keyboard. At the piano his swagger vanished, replaced by an unpretentious and graceful skill. She realized then that the photograph was of Quinn at the piano. The woman was no doubt listening to him, portraits of a love affair with music. She watched him a moment, then closed her eyes. Quinn's music, so vibrant and blue, filled her with delicious melancholy. After a moment she joined him at the piano, bewitched by the metamorphosis. Quinn's eyes never left the keyboard, he treated the instrument with the same grave respect a great climber gives a mountain face. When he asked her to refill their drinks, she did. He motioned for her to join him. They began to laugh together, finishing the drinks, talking quietly. He concluded with "In a Mist," and she put her head on his shoulder, her eyes welling.

On the way downstairs—the living quarters were up, the bedrooms down—he drew a bottle of champagne from the fridge and two glasses from the sideboard. He was very correct. He showed her his study and the bedroom, then led her to the guest room. Loo here, closet there, towels in the cabinet. His music was still in her head, but she could see its spell take leave of Quinn. They finished the champagne sitting on the bed. Before he left to go to his own room he described his friendship with Betsy Dane. All of it was vague, but suggestive. She didn't interrupt him, but it didn't impress her, either. What kind of man was it who wanted you to believe he slept with your mother?

The next day, back in her own flat, she tried to find out. And later, in a mischievous spirit, she repeated the conversation to Quinn:

"Quill? Quill? I don't know any Quill."

"Quinn, Mum. His name is Quinn."

"Australian, you say?"

"American. He's an American writer of mystery stories. I'm told he's quite well known."

"I'm quite sure, although—"

"This would have been some time ago."

"—there was a man called Quill."

"You would've met him in Regent's Park. Peggy's flat."

"A thin man, very tall."

"A large man, very large."

"How curious."

"He seemed to know you quite well."

She sighed. There were so many Americans in London.

"This particular American is conspicuous. He is the size of a wrestler, about forty-five."

"Well, as you know, they come in very large sizes. All

of them are large or extra-large, like eggs. They break easily, too. How do you come to know this Quill?"

"Quinn, Mum. I met him at Peggy's."

"Is he agreeable?"

"He plays the piano."

"Rich?"

"He lives in Chester Square."

"Not sexually irregular?"

She laughed. "As far as I know, no."

"It's something for you to watch out for," she said grimly. "The Americans are very queer these days."

She said, "I'll try."

"Well, Sweet." This was a signal the conversation was ending. The telephone wire hummed. "Anything's possible, of course. I remember once meeting a man at Peggy's, very agreeable man, made me laugh. He knew Great. Or knew of Great. One or the other. Anyway, we talked about your father. It could have been that man, though this was just a passing conversation. I met him *en passant*, as it were. However, it is true that he was agreeable, though I remember him as tall and thin rather than large. And he did make me laugh. Suffering from a cold at the time. Peggy very insistent, you know Peggy, she picks up these strange individuals, many of them Americans, and displays them at her bashes like Meissen horses or suits of armor, depending of course on the American. . . ."

Quinn sent her roses that day and the next and telephoned at strange times, always with unexpected bits of information—the latest joke, a tip on a horse, an interesting lecture at the London School of Economics, or a show at the Tate. They did not speak again of the woman in the photograph or of her mother. Nothing in his manner or conversation indicated that he had another woman in his life, or indeed any existence at all beyond Chester Square, his work, and the friends he called *les compagnons*. She wondered if Carla was a figment of the imagination. There was no evidence of her anywhere, no trace of her at Chester Square, except for the portrait and a few vials of perfume in the loo off his bedroom. She wondered whimsically if this middle-aged man was like the child who invented an imaginary best friend, real enough to the child but unapparent to everyone else. She was a soft touch for mysteries so a week to the day after they met, Tessa moved into Chester Square to share Quinn's life, for a while. And when he told her about his American office and invited her to accompany him to New England, she accepted.

She asked him, "How long can I stay?"

He said, "As long as you like. Or until you get bored."

She said, "I'm never bored."

◇

I listened to all this sitting by the fire in Quinn's study, and when he was finished it was dark outside. Quinn told a good story, adding dialogue, embellishing, inventing what he didn't know, and exaggerating what he did. He was a man of many voices and there was nothing I could say at the end of it. His life was so distant from mine; his was a different country. There was no comment on it I could make. It would take me time to acclimatize myself to his weather— the pressure of it, the music and the mischief, and the restless motion and muscle.

We went upstairs to dress. Quinn's guest room was spacious and wonderfully appointed: a soft leather chair in one corner and a fine big bed, and on the wall a framed poster of the man in the tuxedo, Max Beckmann's self-portrait. There was a dresser with an oval mirror canted down, just so. I put the manuscript on the dresser and the Buddha on top of the manuscript. Buddha was at eye level. When I looked into the mirror I saw the dimpled back of Buddha's head, the crown of his pointed helmet touching my chin. Max Beckmann was behind me, staring morbidly over my right shoulder into the mirror and into my eyes. The poster was from a museum in Frankfurt, though the

42

painting was the property of Harvard. Lowering my head, I looked Buddha full in the face. His eyes were closed in contemplation or in sleep, his lips curving, sealed and expressionless. He had been with me for many years, always guarding my manuscripts. A friend had found him in Cambodia and given him to me as a present. For your peace of mind, she'd said. From me to you for your peace of mind, darling. That was well before the hecatomb, and the invasion and bombing that preceded it. There was a time when Cambodia was like Switzerland. I looked at the back of Buddha's head and again at his strong face. I avoided Beckmann's accusing stare, *Deutsche Kunst des 20. Jahrhunderts*. Speak, Buddha. His face was in neutral but it was potent, like an idling engine. I turned away from Buddha and began to get dressed.

Later, I stood at the window looking down at the driveway. I watched the cars arrive, one behind the other. They all arrived at once, expensive off-road vehicles and dark American sedans easing into the circular driveway. No sound penetrated the walls of Quinn's house. The cars stopped but no one got out. For a moment, until the doors flew open and the people gathered in the headlights—animated, formally dressed, laughing, their cigarettes arching up into the night sky—it looked like a funeral procession.

three

Trailing Quinn into the confusion of the party, I was introduced first to Iris Atherton. She was doing something complicated with her face. I thought she was preparing to weep, but she brought her hand to her throat and sneezed, delicately, making a sharp little cry. She smiled through tears, apologizing for the sneeze, explaining to me that she was allergic to Quinn's cats.

Quinn said, "I don't have any cats, Iris."

"Then it's the dogs," Iris Atherton said.

"There aren't any dogs, either," Quinn said.

"The hell you say," she replied with a guffaw. "Look around!"

"What the blazes do you mean?"

"This ghastly zoo," she said. "Cats and dogs, Quinn's kennels." She guffawed again and turned away.

"Drunk as a goat," Quinn said. "She's out in left field."

We moved on. Quinn smiled confidently, at ease, introducing me to the others as we made our way through the din. Some of the men were introduced by name and occupation, others by name alone; women were meticulously identified, and if they had no identity they were merely "adorable." They were all transplants, slightly out of place in the stony soil of the north country, but struggling noisily to adapt. Many of them were attracted to the public sector, never a breath of scandal, a little jewel box of a government that existed only to serve the people. There were the Churchills, Jay and Deanne, refugees from a great Baltimore law firm, now assistant attorneys general—she civil rights, he criminal justice—and recently photographed by *Town & Country* at their summer place on Nantucket; Art Arnheiter, huge in colorful Icelandic sweater, blue jeans, and riding boots, now selectman in West Bookend; Susan Drinker Bartlett Royster Heatter Gold, Democratic chairman in the northernmost county, whose Independence Day clambake and corn roast was the envy of fund raisers everywhere in the Northeast, and her husband, Gentle Ben, a developer; and poor accident-prone Lacey Doremus, her arm in a sling from a fall from her horse, and boyfriend Sadegh, a graduate student at the university (international relations)—both dressed in leather pants with matching singlet and chukka boots, sleek as sloops turning at anchor. I had met them all at one time or another, always fascinated by their aggressive Good Health. Seeing them again, all in the same room, I felt suddenly deflated; more guests were pushing into the room. There was much conversation of the weather, and the condition of the roads, and the laughable long-distance quality of all their lives. Most of it was a blur, the masculine clothes, the long hair, the tanned faces of the women, and the ruddy complexions of the men. The room was crowded and in motion and I was immediately caught up in it, wondering why I had come; I had never had anything to say to these people. I followed Quinn, who was looking for Tessa.

Then we were standing in front of a smiling red-haired woman.

Quinn took her in a bear hug, then said to me, "The divine Dane. Isn't she adorable?"

She said, "At last. I'm sorry, I was out when you arrived—"

Quinn said, "Where the hell is Marty?"

"She'll be here," Tessa said.

"What?" There was a roar of laughter at the other end of the room. Lacey Doremus was describing how she fell off her horse.

". . . late . . ."

"Bloody outrage," Quinn said.

Tessa moved close to him and said something in his ear.

"They don't understand commitments," Quinn boomed.

"Who doesn't?"

"The children don't. She's adorable but she's too damned young, doesn't understand that when a thing's laid on it's laid on. It's an agreement and not subject to change or amendment. It's this damned . . ." The word was lost in the racket. ". . . and an inability to follow directions, they have no sense of priorities, they're self-absorbed. This is something I've always believed about them."

I turned to Tessa. "What is he talking about?"

"See," Quinn said cheerfully. "He agrees with me."

She said, "It's a theory he has."

Quinn said, "I'm going to leave you two." A few more words were lost. ". . . going to call that gull . . . ridiculous."

"For Christ's sake," I said.

"No, no, she's marvelous gel, though erratic gill." Quinn shook his head and moved off, shouldering his way through the people. He was laughing and shaking hands with them, a politician working the crowd. We watched him go, the people closing in behind him. Tessa took my arm and led me to the corner, where it was quieter. En route she snared drinks for us both, then explained about Marty—who she was, and her relationship to the ménage. I listened carefully, amused. They had met when Marty had given Tessa a ski lesson. Quinn had insisted, it was impossible to live in the north country without knowing how to ski. They had gone to a mountain that had artificial snow and Tessa had spent the day on her backside, hating every minute. A grotesque experience, she said. But they had become friends.

46

On skis Marty was super to watch—not so surprising since that was what she did with her days, ski and teach others to ski. Her body seemed ideally suited to speed or the management of speed, controlled velocity. And it was amusing, watching her and Quinn together, Marty literally running circles around him, carving wide arabesques, skiing with the most complete control, yet somehow giving the impression of abandon, and Quinn plunging down the fall line with no pretense to grace. He did not look as if he were having fun, poor Quinn, until you met him at the base of the mountain, his beard white with snow, his face scarlet, and his eyes glittering, teary, talking like a house afire—this mogul, that drop, Marty alongside him. . . .

Like a fighter escort to a heavy bomber, I said. I described it all with my hands, an aviator describing an adventurous flight. And there would be a certain no-fault elegance to his style (economical in the way a sledgehammer is economical), so monotonous and single-minded; he would rarely tumble. Old Quinn, a man of surprises.

She said, "On the slopes he is a sexy character." And it was sexy watching him, shepherded by Marty, who was super to watch. And of course she always beat Quinn down the hill.

I laughed. "And is she sexy, too?"

"Very," Tessa said. "Moves like a cat."

"I had a cat once. Lazy bastard."

"She is not lazy," Tessa said.

I said, "Quinn calls her a 'marvelous creature.' "

"He does? Well then, she must be."

"Quinn says that his life has taken an erratic turn, with you."

"He has a way with words, that boy." She seemed to flush slightly, and her gray eyes turned inward, disclosing nothing. She said, "His life is erratic with or without me. I'm a passenger, in the boot. Quinn's in the front seat with Carla. What's she like?"

I said, "I've known her for twenty years."

47

"Well then, you must have the complete book. There must be nothing you don't know. You're the Answer Man I've been looking for."

"I like her. She's not easy to know." That was the truth. I said, "She's very involved with her work . . . and her daughter. She balances the two like a lot of women do. Does a good job of it."

"And Quinn?"

"Quinn is a part of her past. She misses him, I think. But he's definitely past, a part of another life. Carla has consciously divided her life into parts. Quinn has no bearing on the present life. Of course Quinn doesn't look at it that way."

Tessa nodded. "That's what I mean. I'm the passenger."

"Come on," I said conversationally.

"Oh yes," she said emphatically. We heard his exuberant laugh. He was on the other side of the room, telling a joke. In a moment there was more laughter, everyone joking, joining in. Tessa watched Quinn with a sweet half-smile that any parent would recognize instantly. It was the smile you made when you watched your child effortlessly charm the company, the one you made when you knew the child wasn't watching.

"What's she like? I mean besides being a marvelous creature and a cat on the slopes."

"Marty?" Tessa thought a moment. She was still watching Quinn. "She is a beautiful young American woman *sans merci*. Men love her."

I laughed. "Why?"

"I don't know," she said. "I don't know anything about men. I wish I did but I don't. It's a legacy, part of my dubious inheritance." She tossed her head and I saw that she was wearing tiny gold earrings. "Maybe they look at her and see something of themselves, the way they'd like to be if they were young and female. I'm sure that's why Quinn likes her, I don't know about the others. Maybe they love her because she threatens them. She threatens them the way their fathers do." She looked at me and smiled. "Is that complicated enough for you?" But she didn't wait for an answer. She continued, "That's all the rage now, threatening men. That's what Marty says. She laughs about it. She says it would be nice to meet one who didn't threaten easily or didn't like to be threatened. Or maybe to meet one who'd just say, 'Go to hell.' "

I thought of my wife. *How would you like to kiss my ass?*

She said, "Of course Quinn doesn't, but that's Quinn. Quinn isn't sensitive in that way. Quinn's indifferent to that sort of thing. He isn't threatened and doesn't like to be threatened but doesn't like *not* being threatened, either." She leaned close to me, grinning. I realized suddenly that she was tight. "You dig?" She added, "Quinn's fun being around but he doesn't let you inside. He gives you a key to the foyer, and you'd better be satisfied with it, and he doesn't care if you're not. There're lots of other rooms, and you don't get a key to any of them. But maybe, with Quinn, the foyer's the most interesting room. Maybe he's like the House of Commons. The most interesting room is the chamber itself, the place where everything is public. The other rooms are just—rooms."

It took me a moment to digest all that, the various threats, fathers' images, and Quinn's rooms; what men saw in Marty, and her attraction to them. This was the aggressive world of single people, where whirl was king and everyone knew too much; it was an anarchy. I wondered what my shrewd wife would make of this terrain, so random and fraught. I thought that Quinn was a lucky man, and never mind the parental smile. Tessa was waiting for me to reply, but I could think of no serious comment to make. I said, "Complicated enough."

She shrugged, making a little disappointed gesture, as if to say, To hell with it, I'm wasting my time. It was very noisy. Someone, not Quinn, was beating on the piano.

I said, "I think you know a lot about men."

49

"Nuts," she said.

"Most of the women I know are smarter than the men."

"More intelligent?"

"Shrewder," I said. "More subtle."

"Lucky you," she said.

"About Marty," I began.

"If she likes you, she'll give you all the keys, invite you inside, let you wander around, browse to your heart's content. She's not like Quinn, there're a lot of small rooms, interesting rooms. She's like a historical building, part of the National Trust, but you've got to respect the furnishings. Do you threaten easily?"

I was laughing. "Never," I said.

"Well then," she said brightly. "It'll be quite a match. And of course you ski, too, so it'll be super. Gosh. You'll be super together, you two."

"I can hardly wait," I said. I had liked Tessa right away and now I liked her more. I said, "Except for one thing. I don't ski."

She looked at me strangely. Was it not a fact that in the north country everyone skied?

"I never learned," I said. "And now I'm too old." The truth was, I had done a little skiing, but I had bad balance; sports was not my métier. I would never be a sexy character on the slopes. And I didn't care for the pretentious crowd that gathered at the mascara mountains. I was convinced that if I ever attempted a downhill run I would break my neck and be paralyzed for life, an object of pity and contempt.

"Good grief," she said, laughing.

"So I don't ski."

"Better not tell her that, she won't understand. She'll think you're a flake, an incompetent. She'll think you frighten easily. And then she'll be merciless."

I took a long swallow of my drink. "Why don't we give her to Quinn, then?"

"That would be very naughty," Tessa said. "And he

doesn't want her, and she won't be given. She's not for sale or rent. So that's not a very good idea at all, no." She touched my arm, it had the effect of softening her words; her eyes widened. "But I see what you're saying, I think." Her accent had grown sharper, almost clipped; it was now located mid-ocean, somewhere between the Back Bay and the Home Counties. She said, "And even if I don't I'll pretend that I do."

"It was a joke," I said stupidly.

She nodded yes.

"And I don't think you're good at pretending."

The party was roaring around us, becoming noisier and rowdier. In the corner, two large men argued. Tessa looked at me and rolled her eyeballs. It looked to be a serious argument. Suddenly there was a crash and a cry of pain, Iris Atherton had fallen or was pushed. Tessa excused herself and rushed to Iris's side. She was sprawled at her husband's feet, grinning maniacally and flailing her arms, drunkenly refusing all assistance. The embarrassed Atherton tried to help. At last she regained her feet, wobbling and making animal sounds. The two large men had stopped arguing and were watching her warily. She put her hands to her mouth and called, *Meeeow!* Then, *Bow-wow!* Atherton had her in a clumsy embrace and they stumbled off.

"Bit early for cabin fever," I said to Tessa. "The winter's barely begun."

"Iris—" she began. But I held up my hand. There was no need to explain, and I didn't want to hear the explanation, whatever it was. Outsiders always got it wrong. Hard drinking in the north country was different from hard drinking anywhere else, at least among those who had leisure. It had different causes, unrelated to work or any kind of neurosis or physical problem or stress. Not so much a question of work as of idleness, and not so much a question of stress as lack of stress. Hard drinking in the north country was a part of the scenery, beauty's accomplice. Twilight was so riotous it had to be contained, this was obvious; hard drinking was as necessary as wearing sunglasses on a bright day. The causes were often mistakenly described as simple boredom or the melancholy of loneliness or fear, but those were not causes, they were symptoms. No wonder the winter was known as "locking-in time." I wondered if Marty was a drinker. Probably she would smoke a little dope, skiers often did, claiming that dope sharpened edges or dulled them; one or the other.

I said to Tessa, "In England, do the women want the men to be vulnerable?"

"No," she said. "They don't."

I said, "In America they do."

"In England, they like them to be stupid. You do not know what stupidity is until you have known a stupid Englishman. And you don't have to look so superior, it's just that England's older and they've had more time."

Quinn waved us over. "A hell of a party."

Tessa put her arm through his and kissed him on the cheek. "Did you see poor Iris?" We watched Ollie Atherton struggle through the door with his wife. He glanced forlornly in our direction and managed a weak wave. The two large men had resumed their argument. The man at the piano was playing a furious boogie.

Swig Borowy tugged at Quinn's sleeve. "Quinn," he said, "let me give it to you again. It's the chance of a lifetime, give those twats a high hard one, we're on Easy Street." He pronounced it "twaaat" to rhyme with "bat."

Quinn looked fondly at Tessa and put his arm around her shoulder. "Sure, Swig."

"Listen," Borowy said.

I said, "Did you get Marty?"

"Didn't," Quinn said. "But she'll be here."

"A high hard one," Borowy said.

"Have you been taking good care of Tessa? This is the first time she's met this mob, doesn't know what to expect."

"She's been taking care of me," I said.

"Nurse Dane," Tessa said. Then, to Quinn, "You've done it again, they're a perfect match, him and Marty."

"That's what I thought," Quinn said.

Swig Borowy leaned close to Quinn. "Look, I did the same thing for your competition." He named a famous writer. "You tie it up, all the loose ends, the original production *and* the residuals, the twats don't know what hit them. The cable, Quinn. How much attention have you paid to the cable?" He smiled knowingly. "The cable's the condominium of the eighties and I'm in on the ground floor. You haven't focused because you're a literary man, can't be bothered with these mundane details. I understand! And that's why Swig Borowy's going to make you rich as the sheikh of Araby."

"I'm already rich," Quinn said.

"That's right," Tessa said.

"I'll parley with them in person, one-on-one. This is Canadian money and it's serious money, this isn't some fly-by-night operation in Ottawa. This is important Montreal money and there's participation by the fucking government, or that's the story, and I have every reason to believe that it's true. It's a production company and they need *properties, comprenez?* Properties with a proven track record. You can be as big a name as R. L. Delderfield, bigger—"

"I'm bigger than Delderfield now. Who the hell is Delderfield?"

"Big," I said.

"A pastoral, forget him," Borowy said. "Thing is, I'm on the inside. I'm way inside, the man who knows the secrets. And I'm sharing. You need me—serious man, experienced, bit of gray in his hair, a drinking man and a good close friend, not like those little twats down from Radcliffe or Oxbridge. Then there's another thing—"

"Please," Tessa said. She hated the word.

"Sorry, Tess. Carried away. It's that agenting used to

be a man's game and a man can't get into it anymore, these young women, aggressive, surly—"

Quinn turned to her. "Swig's going to make me rich and take only twelve and a half percent of the swag. Swig's swag."

"That's it," he said, moving up and down on the balls of his feet.

"Take another swig, Swig."

Borowy turned to Tessa, sensing that Quinn had lost interest. "Best brawl yet."

Quinn said happily, "Everyone's drunk."

Borowy stepped back, working his hands. "So we can talk next week, yes? Sign the papers Tuesday? Burlington Radisson. My treat."

Quinn laughed. "Sure, Swig."

"Thank you kindly," he said formally. Then he cleared his throat. "Uncle Toby has given me his complete assurance, Quinn. No fuckups. It's all laid on, and there's enthusiasm. We just drop the word!" He turned to Tessa. "I must leave, I'm on my way to Montreal. Swell party."

"You're welcome, Swig. But thank Quinn. It's his do."

"Yes, well," he said nervously. "Ha-ha—! Blessings, Your Grace!"

Tessa turned to Quinn, puzzled. "What did that mean?"

Quinn's cold eyes followed the retreating attorney. "Says that he can fix it with the ambassador, his Uncle Toby, to get me a CBE. Says the P.M. owes him one. Or owes his uncle. Uncle got him into gold at the right time. That's the deal. He represents me on the cable, I get the CBE from Her Majesty's Government. The goddamned fool. I handle my own affairs."

I wandered off, maneuvering through the room, feeling nervous and ill at ease. It had been years since I had been in a roomful of people. My life in New England was solitary; even the drinking was solitary. I wished there were

54

only the four of us, Quinn and Tessa and the girl, whatever her name was; at table with four courses of food and four kinds of wine and extravagant talk, lies. She could tell me about moguls and how to avoid them. If the girl was attractive and game I could fall a little in love with her. I looked around, there wasn't a Vermonter in the room; they were New Yorkers or Virginians or midwesterners. I decided that this crowd was unreliable, as exiles generally were unreliable. I remembered hearing that years ago from an influential editor, a friend of presidents. It was given in explanation of the Bay of Pigs.

I headed for the bar, collecting Roy Wendnagle and the Churchills en route. I'd known Roy for years, in Washington and later in the Zone. He had worked for the government in various capacities and was now headmaster of a prep school. We had one drink and then another, and he told me his troubles. They were amusing troubles and he told them with spirit.

". . . son of a bitch weighs three hundred pounds, lives in an ashram in fucking St. Johnsbury. One thing I'll tell you about the teenage gurus. After the chanting of the mantras and the laying on of the hands, *they take no prisoners* . . ." He was talking about his wife's lover, and we were all laughing. ". . . these soldiers of the East, the Wehrmacht of the human potential movement, it's a scorched-earth campaign . . ."

The Churchills moved off, holding hands; they were aggressively affectionate with each other. The room was thick with cigarette smoke and loose bodies, and for a moment they all seemed to move in slow motion, fish under water, glasses levered to mouths and down again, slowly shifting from foot to foot in a languid ballet. Bix Beiderbecke was on the stereo. It looked easy enough, floating in this aquarium. But one would have to be aware of sharks and poisonous crustaceans, and I did not know these fish well enough to assess the danger. There was one woman

55

with us now whose mouth formed little *o*'s when she talked and large *O*'s when she laughed.

"Meet Olene," Roy said. "Olene's with us on the investment. Me'n Quinn, Olene, Susan and Ben, Eddie and Ollie're buying forty-nine percent of two hectares not far from Chambertin—"

"It's in the neighborhood," Olene said.

"It's a hell of a damn fine neighborhood."

"A way to hide your money," Olene said.

"Quinn found out about it," Roy said.

"He's a genius," Olene said.

". . . a wizard . . ."

Willard Lopez joined us to gossip about recent changes in the State Department. He pronounced it Duh-pot-mint. One assistant secretary had been transferred and another obliged to retire prematurely. It was a potential scandal that had somehow not found its way into the newspapers. A miracle, no other word for it. Roy Wendnagle was suddenly silent and I recognized the look. He was trying to clear his memory, to make space for this information.

"Nest of snakes," Willard said. "Vicious."

Roy laughed. "How can it be a nest of snakes? There are no fangs! Can a cobra gum you to death?"

Willard didn't hear, or he didn't choose to hear. He loved the Department of State, even though it was not like the old days, when there were giants in the foreign service. Now there were marketing experts and entrepreneurs from the sunbelt. But everything was going to pieces, why should diplomacy be exempt? Willard said wearily, "Sometimes I just don't see why we don't simply close down the embassies. All representations made from Washington. Relocate the Department at Dulles Airport, send a man or two on every flight, though of course it would be inconvenient for the Nig-Nog countries. Not impossible, though, we could have our own transit lounge, with a bar and a cipher room, at Heathrow and at CDG and Lod. God, I wish I was in Rome."

56

He turned to say something to Roy, but Roy was laughing with Olene.

My glass was empty and I moved to the bar to pour myself another. Willard Lopez followed, his hand lightly on my arm. The hand was slender and manicured; it had been years since I had seen a manicured fingernail. Willard explained that he had but five years remaining in the government, he was up for reassignment. There was a serious question in his mind how he should play it, what to reach for, this being his last waltz for the Foreign Service. Who held the levers of power now? Who were the new men? He grinned at me, as if he thought I knew the answers. I tried to explain that I had been away from Washington. He said confidentially, "I'm thinking about Italy." Sunny Italy for his last assignment, and perhaps retirement in Tuscany. He had friends in Tuscany, where the wine was cheap and plentiful and servants willing. He'd maintained his contacts, he knew every bloody communist labor leader in the country, and he wasn't important enough himself to be kidnapped or knee-shot, except of course no one was safe. Homicidal children, ha-ha, they were shooting shoe clerks in Salerno, why not an average American labor attaché in Rome? Hmmmm?

"Does the Department supply bodyguards?" I asked absently.

"They shoot everybody, even the guards," he replied morosely.

I saw her in the doorway then, a dark girl, dark eyes, black hair full to the shoulders. I knew right away who she was by the familiar way she turned her head, obviously searching for Quinn. Her costume was enchanting. She looked as if she'd stepped in from a stage set somewhere. She wore black boots and a heavy ulster and a man's fedora, the fedora cocked over her right eye. It was a hat of the sort worn by G-men in forties films. She stood motionless, steady as a statue, her eyes flickering over the faces of the crowd, her expression one of mild disapproval. Several people turned to smile at her. Then she saw me and her eyes narrowed. Her cheeks were scarlet from the cold, a flash of color in a dark portrait. She unbuttoned her coat and tipped her hat formally. I touched Willard's arm, excusing myself in mid-sentence.

Marty said, "I'm late."

I said, "We waited."

four

She kissed me lightly on the cheek, as if we were old acquaintances, perhaps cousins. She did not remove her coat but stood looking at me, then over my shoulder at Quinn's horde. She seemed ill at ease, though somehow above it all. Tentatively, I handed her my drink and she took a quick sip, her eyes restless and in motion over the rim of the glass. She smiled her thanks, raising her eyebrows, murmuring, "What a mob." I nodded, watching the amusement in her eyes; it was either amusement or fright. I wondered what it was that she found unsettling. Perhaps it was only her own incongruity. She was the youngest person in the room and dressed for a beat in the Yorkshire Dales, all she lacked was a shotgun. She glanced down at the hem of her coat, then at me. She said, "I guess I should really say hello to Tessa and Quinn, tell them I'm here." I said she could do that, if she wanted to run the gantlet to get to them.

"I can't," she said, laughing.

"Then don't," I said.

"Will they mind?"

"They won't mind."

"I have a friend here." Her eyes roamed the room. She

described the friend, willowy and blond, very nice, somewhat shy. "Look for one the opposite of me," she said.

"She's gone, I saw her go." This was true, there had been a blond young woman at the party. I'd watched her slip inconspicuously away with her escort, a blond young man, from the look of him an Austrian.

"I was afraid of that; this isn't her scene at all, and she didn't want to come. Did she have a good time?"

"I suppose she did," I said. "There's plenty of champagne to drink."

"She doesn't drink," Marty said thoughtfully. "She's in training for the trials. She only came because I asked her to, in case . . ." Marty neglected to finish the thought, then shrugged and pointed to the stairs leading to the basement, Quinn's study, and the billiards room, and said that if I hated crowds as much as she did we could go sit on the bottom step, away from things. It was not sociable but it would be quiet and we could talk and get to know each other. She had heard a lot about me, she confided, actually too much, more than she wanted to know, most of it from Quinn. After a while she didn't know who I was, a real person or a character from one of his books. She spoke rapidly and I knew she was nervous. She peeked around my shoulder and shuddered, her dark eyes restless under the brim of the fedora, fixing now on one part of the room, now on the other, finally coming back to me. Actually, she said, it wasn't the crowds that bothered her. She liked crowded parties, the noisier the better. "It's the—" She hesitated, imagining that she had gone too far. Quinn, after all, was my good friend.

"Bores," I said.

"Right," she said, "bores. And I've met all these bores before. Have you?" She put her hand on my arm, her grip tight enough for me to feel her fingers. Around us voices rose in a frantic babble. I said I'd fetch a bottle of champagne and two glasses and join her on the stairs. "Or are you in training, too?"

She shook her head.

I said, "Don't go away."

"Don't be long," she said.

Settled at last, we reconnoitered, facing each other in the half-light of the stairwell, the champagne poured, sipped, and poured again. I complimented her on her costume and she rolled her eyes. She'd had no time to change, she wasn't able to leave the slopes until five, and it was so darned *far* to Quinn's house. In the north country, everything was two hours away from everything else. . . .

No, I said; I was serious. I said I found the fedora a wonderful touch. Where did you get it? I bought it, she said, pleased, naming a boutique in the mall at Winooski. Too expensive, but everyone had to have a personal signature. The fedora was hers. We talked of this and that, and when she found something that interested or amused her she canted her head to the right and raised her chin, looking down her nose like a blithe Humphrey Bogart; it was an oddly ribald pantomime. It seemed there were no barriers between us; there had been none from the moment she kissed me. I laughed without knowing why, taking my time with the champagne, happy to be there with her.

I have no idea at what age men receive their images of women. No doubt they commence at first light and continue forever; the later images only reinforce the earlier ones. Once I made a list of all the women I'd fallen for, with what I conceived to be their salient characteristics, faults and virtues. Beneath the name of each woman—there were not many—I wrote various vital statistics, concluding with a little explanatory essay, much as a historian might do with a nation. I thought I could find common ground and therefore come to know myself better. It seemed reasonable enough at the time—to understand oneself by the women one had loved, like defining a president by his cabinet or a kingdom by its monarchs. In its way it would be like looking into a cracked mirror. But I never found any common ground, except in the most general way. This was disappointing, like discovering that the only shared characteristic of Vermont and New Hampshire was that they were both located on the Canadian border. In any case, the only characteristic the women shared was that they were fond of me. They knew me, as different nationalities of a region know a common language. Not much to go on, I thought then; as aids to self-analysis, women were useless. Later, I had second thoughts. The variety of women I had loved was itself an illuminating fact. And, no buts about it, much later I concluded that they were *very* different women, each from the others; they must have been, for all of them eventually married and none of their husbands was anything like me.

I poured more champagne. She was talking easily in a soft, unselfconscious voice, telling me what she did at the mountain and describing her career as a student, hinting at confusion in the ivory tower. She had graduated in June, bored and irritated with classes and learning, and frightened of the city. Then a man she knew offered her a job as a ski instructor and she thought, Why not? It was hard work and she could be outdoors and stay in shape. And since she was having a wee fling with the man at that time, it seemed a convenience; and she did love to ski and was good at it. She loved the north country, too, though it was important not to fight it. You had to understand the flow and go with it, but that was obvious, everyone knew it. She was a better skier than her blond friend, which was why she didn't have to be punctilious about training. The trials would be fun, and with a little bit of grit she ought to win something, perhaps the slalom, her best overall event.

She talked on about the trials, but I wasn't listening. I was gawking at her. She was so good-natured and fresh; her mirror was in no way cracked or distorted. She was proudly open. Most of the women I knew were thick with nuance and had histories as complicated as the Balkans'. They were possessed by the facts of the past, "comfortable" with themselves, or so they said. So they insisted. It was necessary to handle these women with care. A man had to

62

fit in between the nuances, and the boundaries were so tangled and in opposition to one another that the wise man stepped cautiously, a map always at hand. The mirror threw back conflicting images, often two or more images at once. Exploring the past with such a woman was like walking through a minefield. There was so much to contend with, and so much to remember, if a man was to protect himself. They wanted everything. Women had elephants' memories and men as a rule did not, so the struggle was unequal; it was as if one lawyer went up against a firm of lawyers, all of them with photographic memories. And of course a woman was always her own judge, and a hanging judge usually. And they didn't understand independence and the frequent necessity to *forget*, though it was true that my wife had urged me to go to Quinn's specifically to "forget about things." An insightful woman, my wife; she was the exception that proved the rule. Yet each year their intransigence and bellicosity increased, they knew so much. . . .

I was thinking of these things while watching Marty. She was not old enough to remember chapter and verse, thank God. Her memory would be a perfect small room in an unfinished mansion, the room filled with pretty, unbreakable objects. . . .

She drained her champagne and leaned forward, giggling suddenly, pulling at an earring. She balanced the empty champagne flute on the crown of her head, the base disappearing into her thick black hair. I wondered how she saw herself. In moments of repose, her mind an empty stage, which characters swept in from the wings? She slowly tipped her head and the flute slipped, falling, sluggish as a redwood. She caught it in midair and held it out for a refill.

She said that at college she began by studying physics but ended with history. However, neither discipline suited her. She was not suited to discipline, period, except the discipline of staying healthy and in shape. Somehow it seemed a natural trajectory, from the physicist Feynman to the historian Braudel. How could anyone forget Feynman, that

63

loon, who maintained that everything was known and all that remained for humankind was to put the pieces together correctly. Then Braudel, stoned on facts. No fact too eensty-weentsie or obscure to memorize and collate, and there were as many facts as there were grains of sand on a beach. She sighed. Pessimistic old men. There was so much to learn, and what was the consequence? So she stayed healthy and in shape, the best armor against bad vibrations.

We were facing each other on the stairs. She had taken off her hat and ulster and put them on the step next to her. Without them she looked déshabillé. I picked up the hat and put it on her head at a rakish tilt, the brim snapped down. She took it off at once, scowling when she mussed her hair.

She said, "You weren't listening."

"I was," I protested. I was surprised that she knew Braudel, a hero of mine, a poet of the commercial life; I was attracted to his theories of geography. The other name meant nothing to me, but I didn't think he sounded like a loon.

"No," she said. "But it doesn't matter. It's boring. I don't care about it anymore, and I'm happy to be where I am and doing what I'm doing." She smiled brightly. "What are you doing here?"

I said, "I got lonely."

She looked at me, interested. "Quinn said you were trying to finish a book."

"That, too," I said.

"A book on the war," she said. "Why did you get lonely, you had your book? Quinn's never lonely when he's writing a book."

"Lucky Quinn," I said.

"How lonely did you get?" She leaned toward me, curious.

I wanted to tell her in detail, describe for her the oceanic emptiness of my life in the north country; but that was a step into a mine field of another kind, and it was too soon. Often I had ruined things by my haste, and she was so young. So I set out to define for her the perimeters of my north country, its particular features, geographical and psychological, the forests that surrounded my house, the animals that inhabited the forest, the western range rising in seven different shades of blue, my habitual attendance at the evening news, and of course the memories that surrounded it all. But I did a bad job of it. The way I explained it, my world sounded attractive and welcoming, though undeniably austere, governed by the various inalienable laws of nature. Of course there was the book, too, but it existed in another realm altogether. I filled her glass with champagne.

She nodded when I finished, saying that it sounded fine to her. A fine life. Why didn't I ski?

"I never learned," I said. This was not strictly true.

She said, "I'll give you a lesson."

I said, "I have bad balance."

She said, "You'd like it better, where you are, if you skied. When you ski, you get out of yourself; or sometimes just the opposite, you can go way inside. It depends on what you want."

I smiled at that.

"Good," she said, taking the smile for agreement.

"I do cross-country," I said.

"We can do that, too."

"Honestly," I said. "I have bad balance."

She looked at me. "Why did you go to the war?"

"They sent me," I lied.

She said, "Do you know what D. H. Lawrence said about war? It was in *Women in Love*. He said, 'Why do men go to war? Because the women are watching.' " She considered that a moment, then asked me if I thought it was true.

I hesitated. Of course it was not Lawrence of Nottingham but Lawrence of Arabia, and not *Women in Love* but *Seven Pillars of Wisdom*. It was a quotation I knew well, it being a favorite of my wife. I said I guessed it was partly true.

"So women are responsible?"

65

"God, no," I said.

"Well then?" She looked at me closely, as if she were making up her mind about something. There was so much I wanted to explain and so much I couldn't. The war's mirrors were cloudier than any woman's. The details were simple enough to grasp but the experience was not and the meaning of it even less so. Certainly, it was time to invoke Einstein's great rule. Why were we so happy to be there? In the war zone things stood at opposite poles, and for many of us it was a flight from responsibility; perhaps the same was true for those in charge. I told her that. As reporters we were in the middle of it, literally the middle; it was not a difficult war to describe, from the middle. In fact, it lent itself to aggressive reportage. And in some ways it was true, we went because the women were watching; we were always conscious of women's eyes.

She cocked her head. "No man I knew went."

I smiled. "You're too young."

"My brother didn't," she said. "None of his friends did. My dad offered round-trip tickets to Canada or Sweden or any other place. But my brother went to grad school instead."

"Because the women were watching," I said.

She smiled. "Maybe."

"If Lawrence was right," I said. "I went because the women were watching and your brother didn't go because the women were watching."

"You place too much importance on women," she said.

I laughed at that.

"True?"

"Nothing truer was ever spoken," I said.

"Poor you," she said, still smiling.

I smiled back, pouring more champagne, just a little because the bottle was almost empty. We had gradually moved closer to each other, our legs touching, then our shoulders. We were suddenly holding hands, continuing the talk where everything seemed to have a double meaning. Upstairs Quinn had begun to play the piano. The chords reached us faintly, indistinct, soft as mist. He was playing the first bars of a very old blues. Our faces were only inches apart and I thought she had the blackest, clearest eyes I had ever seen. She removed my glasses and put them on the step beside her. It was as if we'd reached a high plateau after an hour's hike. No hardship and no wilderness and no footsore afternoons under a hostile sun, no struggles through the unfriendly underbrush. We had gotten there too quickly. Somehow we hadn't earned our way, we hadn't prepared the ground. Marty was smiling in an odd way and I knew she was thinking the same thing. So after a moment's silence I commenced a little parody of small talk—restaurants of the north country and the Burlington theater. The location of the most diversified salad bar and the thickest New York strip. Where Ibsen was bad and where he was good. I moved the conversation to Tessa and Quinn, a love affair that was doomed. Hard times, hard times ahead. Quinn's house was no place to pursue a love affair, one was never *alone*.

The way we are now, I said.

She said, So you came here to get back to basics.

That's right, I said.

And do you? Did you?

I try, I said.

It doesn't sound to me like, like you try very hard. I don't think you try hard at all, she said, laughing.

And you? I asked. Where do you go from here?

Who knows? she said.

You won't stay here forever, I said.

Colorado, she said suddenly. It's so big. There's so much there. If you know how to ski the north country you can ski anywhere. That's the great thing about the north country, it really sets you up for the West. In Colorado there's a nation of virgin trails and as a matter of fact they aren't *trails*, that's the point. These are slopes, shoulders, whole ranges, yours for the asking. You say, Here, let me have some of that! They say, Sure! How much do you want? How much do you think you can take? She laughed at her invention, her hand closing around mine. And if you can manage to hire a chopper, so much the better. Have you ever flown in a chopper? You can go out where no one's ever been before, it's so cool. That sound, slap*slap*slap*slap*, and then setting down on a saddle, hopping off, and the chopper whirling away. Oh, I love it! See, this is the thing. There's nothing holding you back, and you know that whatever the mountain deals out, you can handle because you've skied New England. You've skied *trails* so you can ski slopes.

Yes, I said.

I've only been there once, but we were really into it, my boyfriend and me.

I said, "Listen to Quinn." He was replicating Jimmy Yancey. I started to say something else, then didn't. I was going to ask her about her boyfriend, and where the helicopter took them in spacious, cool Colorado. Vail? Aspen? Telluride? Instead, I began to describe the music, Chicago rent-party piano, and the men who played it. It was music drenched in sadness and fatalism, and the dignity that comes with the certain knowledge that the past is prologue. It was antique music, and the old black men who made it were dead before Marty Neher was born. I wondered if it was an advantage, knowing nothing of that.

She was humming softly, not the song Quinn was playing. I listened to his music, remembering the first time I entered the Zone, flying in high. Someone had a portable tape recorder playing Bunny Berigan. A swinging tune, he'd shouted, for a swinging war! He was drunk and the stewardess finally took away the tape recorder and turned it off; and suddenly the cabin was silent except for the heave of the engines as the plane banked sharply. There was the light blue of the South China Sea, then the green of the Delta, shimmering in the early-morning light, so level it seemed to go on forever. What a killing ground, I thought. There were rivers everywhere and small market towns, but there was no sign of war. I wanted to know everything about this nation—its borders, highlands, lowlands, interiors, coasts, ports of entry, its provinces and districts, lakes and cities. Driving in from the airport, my senses stretched tight after twenty-six hours on the plane, I noticed first the odor of food. There were open-air kitchens on every street corner. The streets were thick with people, some of them walking or riding bicycles, many more on Hondas. Always Hondas. I wondered who held the import license. The noise was terrific. Soldiers walked hand in hand, ogling the girls in *ao dais*. All those people. In time we would come to describe them as one person, a single representative, "the Vietnamese."

Her back was resting against the banister now, her legs stretched out on the step, shoes off, her toes touching the opposite wall. I was sitting on the step above, my legs a tunnel for hers. I wondered what she was thinking about, and if I was as new to her as she was to me, and if she had the same urge to exploration. I poured the last drops of champagne, and we silently toasted each other. Quinn had shifted styles and was driving hard out of "Blue Skies." Marty closed her eyes, smiling. I looked up dreamily and was startled to see Tessa leaning over the first-floor railing. She quickly withdrew, embarrassed. My eyes were so bad, she was gone before I could say anything. But she told me later that she was holding her breath, watching us as she would watch aerialists, wondering when the spell would break and we would tumble to earth. She said she was mesmerized by the stillness surrounding us. The only sign of the physical world, or of any world beyond ourselves, was the infinitesimal movement of my foot, beating time to Quinn's music.

five

Rain lashed at the windows. The north country was flooding. Radio broadcasts supplied the news: water to the south, snow to the north, airports closed, power failures general. Secure and dry in Quinn's house, Tessa and I had spent the afternoon reading and listening to the opera on the CBC. Quinn was in his study, working. I was reading a book on the unlucky lives of American poets, and every now and then I looked up and smiled. In the north country, rain usually meant gloom inside and out. But somehow in Quinn's spacious living room the weather was only a bloody nuisance; in fact, the driving rain was picturesque.

Marty had left early, before I was awake, for her morning run. She was undeterred by rain, happy to be on Quinn's road. The road wound up the hill for another mile, then became little more than a wide track; in the last century it had been a logging road, and a determined hiker could follow it for five miles through the uninhabited back country. We had stayed up very late, utterly alone in the big bedroom on the second floor, and she had not bothered to wake me; nor had she left a note. When she finished her run, she drove to work. And joined us at six, tired but cheerful; two hours south, in the high country, the rain had turned to snow and the skiing would be fine, though a little sticky.

Quinn did not know what had happened between us the night before, and that made him nervous. I volunteered nothing. Quinn lit the fire and we had drinks standing around the fireplace, making bets when the rain would stop and the snow begin. We did not dine until ten. At table Quinn talked about his career. He was expansive, defining his writer's life. Mostly it was a speculation about roads not taken. None of these untraveled roads now seemed to him very interesting. He had no serious regrets and no disappointments and of course no remorse. He seemed to go from success to success and could not imagine beginning again. He often wondered what he could do if he were unable to write and couldn't imagine. He would make a passable bartender and a superb mechanic and a good enough café pianist, but life without Tom Plumb would be no life at all. Quinn said, "He is a hell of a man but I wouldn't want to be him. He is great to read about, not so great to *be*. Of course he is my closest friend," Quinn concluded, "except him," meaning me.

"You," he said, looking at Marty. "It's decision time for you, now."

She said, "No, it isn't."

"What are you going to do, teach snowplows to stockbrokers for the rest of your life? Romance those overage Austrians who have such a good time with the ladies from Newton and Darien?"

Tessa said, "Shut up, Quinn."

He said, "It's irresponsible. You're letting down the side."

Marty laughed thinly. "Whose side?"

"The future," Quinn said. "You could be a judge," he added thoughtfully. "Manager of the New York Giants?" Quinn fixed her with a speculative eye. He said that much was expected of her. She was on the fast track and there were no exits, however much she might want them. Of course she might have the bad luck to want to be a stenographer or, God forbid, a housewife or mother after a year or two on the slopes. No way, José. She'd be obliged to become a corporation executive or airline pilot or manager of the New York Giants. It's impossible, Quinn said, your situation. The sisters'll force you. You've been chosen to discharge the legacy of two millennia of shame. Two millennia of misrule." He laughed loudly.

"Stenography is not my line," she said.

Quinn glanced at me. "Lucky you," he said.

"Or motherhood or housekeeping. And I don't like predictions."

"Listen," Quinn said. "How about this: author's agent and mouthpiece. If that half-wit Swig Borowy can make a living at it, why not you? You were an English major. Of course your daddy's not ambassador. That helps, when it comes to destabilizing things."

She glared at Quinn. "As a matter of fact, it was physics. And after physics, it was history. Like most men, you've got your facts wrong. Men have been trying to predict things for me all my life. They act as if I owe them something, as if I'm the favorite in the Belmont stakes and if I don't come in winners I've let them down and they've lost a bundle. It's just another kind of condescension. It's a way of holding on to you, playing prophet; and then playing patron. Stick with me, baby; with my help, you'll get somewhere. You think we'll come to depend on you as court ladies of the Middle Ages depended on astrologers. I don't know why you're so hell-bent to do it. It's old, old stuff." Her gaze shifted to include me. "What do you get out of it? What's the prize? Does it make you feel virtuous?"

I reached for the wine, hoping that this did not foreshadow a discussion of the women's movement. My wife and I had devoted many hours to the subject. It was like Gettysburg—there was nothing more to be said about it; the ground had been exhaustively surveyed, the tactics analyzed, the casualties counted, the books written; and the good side won. I was bored with it in my own house and did not want to be bored with it in Quinn's. I thought among tedious subjects it was rivaled only by golf. I looked at Tessa and raised my eyebrows, but she was sitting back in her chair, grinning, enjoying the show. They went at it through the dessert, both of them strident now; even Quinn had become humorless.

Finally Tessa called for silence and poured poire, concentrating on it as if it were nitroglycerin. We all watched her carefully. I said something about the rain. Quinn switched on the stereo, then brought another bottle to the table. This was one of his exotic liqueurs, and he prattled on about it, lighting cigars for himself and for me. He ostentatiously offered one to Marty, who accepted with a forced smile. Presently we were laughing again.

Quinn urged Tessa to tell one of her Mum stories.

She asked, "What kind of story?"

Quinn said, "One of the political ones."

She nodded and began, "Mum had a liaison once with a vice-president."

"No," Quinn said. "Not that one."

"It's an interesting story," Tessa protested.

Quinn turned to me. "It's your average everyday story of sexual potency equalling political power, or maybe it's the other way around. I've forgotten. There are several versions."

Marty said, "Tell the story you want."

Tessa said to me, "Mum's American but she's lived in England for so long she might as well be English. Same with me. There are stories of all shapes and sizes, any moral you want—"

I said, "Sexual anarchy."

Tessa grinned broadly, standing now behind Quinn's chair, her hands on his shoulders. She knew exactly the story to tell. She said, "During the war she loved a famous correspondent—"

"O Christ," Quinn said. "Not that one."

Marty said, "Be quiet, Quinn."

"Goddamned endless story," Quinn muttered.

"—she was working in the OSS then and met him in Paris under agreeable circumstances. They got on well, it was a genuine love affair, and they briefly considered getting married, except on the weekend they were to go to Saint Philippe du Roule—no Army chaplain for Mum—he was obliged to tell her that he had a dose of the clap. Ver-ry sorry, he said, he was rilly sorry but she'd been extremely pretty and willing, this nurse at the 8th Field Hospital. Mum was angry for a day but couldn't stay angry because he was a highly amusing man, always in disarray, and an excellent correspondent. He was always able to make her laugh and of course that's a great prize. And I think she was not, in her heart, very eager to get married. Anyhow, after the clap, marriage to the famous correspondent was out of the question. 'A violation of the Conventions,' Mum said. They drifted apart and at the end of the war were in different theaters. She didn't see him again for twenty years until quite by chance she came across him one country weekend. While the host and hostess knew they were acquainted, they had no idea how well. There were ten to dinner, and Mum had two yellow cocktails—that's what she calls martinis, 'yellow cocktails'—before dinner and much wine during dinner and a cognac after dinner and she found herself talkative. The famous correspondent, who was by then a very famous correspondent, was uncommunicative at table and went to bed at midnight, the other guests leaving shortly thereafter. The host and hostess went reluctantly to bed, leaving Mum alone in the library with a last cognac and a book. Well, she thought, what the hell, why not?"

She said, "Seeing the famous correspondent again brought back the good times they'd had together, and they'd had a lot of good times, and the unfortunate denouement to their 'engagement'—she thought of him as her former fiancé. So she poured a second cognac and, a glass in each hand, mounted the stairs to his room. She knew where he was, she was always careful to get a layout of wherever she was staying—a habit, she said, from her OSS days. She always sits with her back to the wall in a restaurant and when she drives keeps an eye on the rearview mirror. She also fancies herself qualified in small arms, but that's another story.

"She knocked on the door and tiptoed in. *Pssst! Darling, it's me!* The famous correspondent stirred and sat bolt upright. Mum sat on the edge of his bed, grinning, and handed him the cognac. She knew she was damned attractive still, she'll be an attractive woman when she's ninety. She unbuttoned her blouse while she talked, Mum was never coy. As she was doing her little striptease his eyes narrowed and he moved away from her. She said, *Alumni privileges, darling. I've come to enjoy my alumni privileges.* He was almost falling off the bed now, looking at her with—she thought it was fear mixed with desire. He said, 'No, no, this is not possible.' She said, 'Nonsense, darling. Class of '44. It's not nonsense, it's the real thing. It's 1944 and we're in glorious Paris and you've yet to visit the disgusting 8th Field Hospital.' He said again, 'No.' She had her blouse off now and was undoing her bra. She touched him on the cheek, he was still marvelously handsome, though his looks were unusual. His face was battered and lined as a road map, deep lines under the eyes. Mum said you could plant beans in the furrows of his forehead, and of course his voice was rough. 'No, Betsy,' he said again, but his manner was not convincing and her hand stayed where it was. Mum was never one to believe that no was a satisfactory answer to anything. He sounded as if he meant what he said and she couldn't believe it. In the old days he'd loved to fuck her. That was what he called it and at that time men usually didn't. He loved doing it, anytime, anyplace. They'd fucked on army cots and in the backs of jeeps and in foxholes and once underneath a tank and more than once in the Bois de

Boulogne, as well as in the large four-poster in her apartment on the Île Saint-Louis. He took her hand away from his chin and put it back in her lap, holding her wrist, she said, as if it were a cold lamb chop. He didn't move toward her but stayed away on the edge of the bed. 'Darling,' she said, smiling. She has a wonderful smile, a dimple on each cheek, and eyes that could've launched the Royal Navy. Men have been known to fall in love with the smile. She put her hand on him, thinking of 1944 and the way it had been. She was falling in love with him again and it was inconceivable that he would not requite her. She reached under the covers and leaned toward him, her breasts brushing his rigid arm. She whispered something in his ear and smiled again. But he pushed her hard, away from him.

" *'For Christ's sake, I'm gay. Now you get the hell out of here!'*

"And she did, poor Mum. But at her own pace. Not jumping up in surprise or disgust or humiliation. She simply cocked her head the way she often does, staring at him a moment. He would not meet her eyes. Then she slowly replaced her bra and her blouse and stood up, smoothing her skirt. And she leaned down quickly to pat him once, there; and then she left, quickly."

Quinn's shoulders moved under Tessa's fingers, and she must have realized that her nails were digging into his skin because she released him right away. Quinn did not look at her. He said, "That's a hell of a story. A hell of a *story!* I think I can use that in the next novel."

Tessa said to no one in particular, "Mum said he had 'pleading eyes.' That's what she called them, 'pleading eyes.' Poor baby, she felt so sorry for him. Twenty years before, during the Second World War, she'd just loved him to death." She went and stood stiffly in front of the fire, her stockings glittering.

Quinn vaulted out of his chair, gesturing with the bottle. Marty and I followed. His vitality filled the room. He lumbered to the stereo and presently Bix Beiderbecke's horn began to cry. Tessa sank to the floor and sat there limply, looking at Quinn. Then she brightened and stretched languidly on her side, beckoning to him. She wanted him to lie down next to her. "Come on, Quinn! Make a spoon!"

"In a minute," he said. He'd lit a cigarette and was leafing through his phonograph records, complaining that one was lost or stolen.

She looked at me. "You said you wanted sexual anarchy."

I nodded.

"She's a survivor, isn't she? My mum?" Tessa smiled bleakly, then glanced at Quinn, who was still fussing with the phonograph records. "Come on, Quinn! A spoon!"

"Someone's pinched my Bunk Johnson."

"So put on the Brahms and come here."

"You can't keep anything in this place, goddamned people in and out. It's like Victoria Station." She began to laugh, listening to Quinn's inventory of complaint. He said he would establish his own security system, armed guards at the doors. . . . Then she wasn't laughing anymore but staring through tears at the fire. Marty rose and kneeled beside her. They were together a moment, looking like sisters, murmuring, Tessa's head concealed in the arch of Marty's arm. Quinn was silent now, sorting records. A sharp look from Marty told me not to interfere, and they retreated into the dining room. I had no intention of interfering; this was so theatrical and unbuttoned I did not know how to react.

"Women," Quinn muttered, settling into his chair. "They'll say any damned thing, tell any story. Can you imagine telling a story like that one? She cried the last time, too." He shook his head, indicating either disgust or admiration, it was hard to tell which. He laughed suddenly and poured fresh drinks. "What do you want to hear, now that they've stolen my Bunk?"

I said I didn't care. Bix, any of the Chicagoans. I wondered how much of Tessa's story was true. Then I wondered how much of it Tessa believed to be true, and what she made of it. Well, the tears were an answer to that.

Quinn glanced over from the stereo, suddenly solemn. "It's something Tessa has to deal with—Mum—which she does by telling the stories. It's nothing to get damp about, that just upsets her. She tells the stories to people she believes will not repeat them. And of course you would not do that, being a gentleman of discretion. And because if you do I will cut off your left one with a rusty knife."

I held up both hands. "You were rough on her."

Quinn cocked an eyebrow. "She's not a child. I do my friends the favor of saying exactly what I think. As for the other one, if she wants to live in a man's world she'd better get used to our way of talking. I won't patronize them."

"I'm like a needle on a compass," Marty was saying, "swinging from north to south and back again. . . ."

I was looking at Quinn but listening to her.

". . . I can't choose." She was talking about a career now. "I can't choose and I don't want to be wrong. Afraid of making the wrong choice so I don't make any choice at all, just go along, ticktock like a watch . . ."

"Screwed-up families . . ." Quinn said.

"What?"

"May be one of the great differences, people who come from screwed-up families and people who don't. My mother told me that. I never believed her, but she was right. They like things complicated and don't understand it when they're not. They'll take a perfectly simple thing and make it complicated just so they can understand it. They're not like us."

I looked at him and laughed.

"Your life and mine," Quinn said. "Simplicity itself, and it arises from our normal, stable families. Our parents, married a lifetime. To each other."

"Absolutely," I said. Quinn often walked a thin line between absurdity and insight, and sometimes in Quinn they were the same thing. The women were still tête-à-tête. Marty was talking and Tessa was listening, but her words were so muted I could not hear them. "I like Tessa," I said. "What about Carla?"

"She understands all about it," Quinn said. "I've explained it to her and she understands it. Explained it early on." He gave the women a furtive look and leaned across the table. "She ought to understand it, I've explained it often enough. With Carla, it's as if we're married. Same's you. Same thing exactly, except we don't happen to live together or see each other. Love Carla, always will except we couldn't work it out. Sometimes you only get one chance and we missed the chance. And that's just tough titty." He leaned closer. "And maybe in the beginning I fell for Tessa, and I admit that the arrangement that Carla and I have is a little peculiar and takes some study to fathom. But that's what we have and it's stood the test of time, the only test that means a damn. All of the others have understood it, but Tessa doesn't understand it. Because that's the way it is and it's not going to change. I don't want any changes, I've grown comfortable with the thing as it is." Quinn was up now and pacing, glaring at the women in the other room. "The other ones understood it, damned if I know why she can't. Sometimes they try to crowd the hell out of you."

"Well, I like her."

"So do I, a lot. I don't know what happens to them though. They go out of whack. They have no restraint." He went to the window and stood a moment, listening to the rain. "I like living alone, it's relaxing. Then after a while I don't like it and I get someone in. I like it when no one's here. When I'm alone I can go to bed at ten and get up at six and begin the writing at once. Or the reverse. Sometimes I just read all night. Sometimes I write in my journal. That's all right for a while and then I don't like it anymore. I meet a woman somewhere, agreeable woman, and I want to find out more about her and before you know it she's moved in." He shook his head in dismay. "But when a woman's here we have to have the parties and do the drinking and when I'm doing the drinking I'm not plotting the novels. It makes me damned insecure. And they make dates for you that you don't want. It got so I was having to leave the House of Commons at *three,* for Christ's sake, because she'd arranged—"

"You still going there?"

"Sure," he said. "Better than the British Museum." Quinn's habit was to visit the House of Commons when it was in session. He got story plots from the debates or said he did. Friends who had seen him in the Strangers' Gallery claimed he slept. When he was in London his routine was to lunch at his club, two martinis and a bottle of claret with the game pie, then walk to Westminster. He made notes on the back of an envelope, listening to the debates.

"But the thing is," Quinn went on, "she tries to organize me. She clutters my house with flowers. When she's reading she uses the OED and never puts the volumes back where they belong. The other night she looked out the window and said apropos of nothing, 'Do you know what they're doing now, all of them? Screwing. That's what they're doing all over North America. Bouncing beds.' " He paused and sighed loudly. "And I'm forty-four."

I didn't get the last. "What?"

"Years old!" Quinn boomed. He nodded at the women. "It's better here than it was there. There aren't any flower shops here, thank God. But she's tried to redecorate the office, and the other night there was some anxiety over my body and what I was doing to it—"

"It's not that," I said.

"No, it isn't. But let's pretend for a moment that it is. My liver—"

I said, "We both like to drink."

"There was some conversation along those lines."

"Well, she's not dumb."

"No, she's smarter than a tree fulla owls. But she tried to get smart with me. One of those serious heart-to-hearts that they love to have when they haven't anything better to do. I got mad as hell. It's the thing that Carla never did, ever." I nodded gravely. There was something almost medieval about Quinn's "arrangement," the two of them sequestered in adjoining castles, exchanging letters but never meeting. No responsibilities on either side, except to cherish what they had had, once. Quinn's books were identically dedicated, "To C." At times I considered the arrangement an act of profound idealism, at other times the reverse; whichever, Quinn was satisfied. And in her way, Carla was, too. For this and other reasons, Quinn would never marry. He said loudly, "I like Tessa a lot. Hear that?" He looked over at her, scowling. Then he turned back to me and said quietly, "But it isn't the way it was."

"Before."

"Before she got pushy, a lot of questions about Carla and me. Carla's never critical, never pushy, we understand each other too well. And of course the situation's different, I acknowledge that. Been through the fires, we have. That's got its disadvantages too, but what the Christ, if you're our age and the thing's *okay*. We know what we had and we refuse to spoil it. . . . " His voice was rising and he was looking again at Tessa, who was staring back at him blankly, her chin in her palm. "If it's okay you stick with it because turbulence is the enemy of art. Same's children. 'The pram in the hallway is the enemy of art.' And there's disaster all around with guys who've thought the grass was greener. And it wasn't, after the first month. Not that life is ever completely satisfactory, no." I smiled. Tessa had come up silently behind Quinn and now put her hand on his head.

I said, "You don't understand about the women and I'm here to set you straight. They only want to put you in touch with your own feelings."

"Is that it?"

"Absolutely," I said. "It's a service they perform."

Quinn said, "God bless them."

"You're out of touch with your feelings. It's obvious. There's been talk."

"Is that right?" We were both laughing now and Quinn

made a face as Tessa put her fingers around his throat. He leaned forward and spread his hands, an entreaty. "You can't do the drinking, write the novels, practice the psychotherapy, and be in touch with the feelings."

"It is awkward," I said.

"And sleep with the women."

"Yes," I said.

"At one and the same time," he said.

Tessa said, "Ha!"

Quinn nodded confidently. "Om," he purred. In an instant he was on his feet and circling the room like a great disheveled cat, flapping his arms in time to Beiderbecke's horn. Outside, the rain continued to drive against the windows. "Ommmmmmmmmmmmm." He buttoned his shirt and snatched the bottle from the table, still moving in circles. Chanting, his head thrown back, Quinn suddenly bounded to the fireplace, bowed to the fire, pirouetted once, and crashed to the floor. "It's spoon time!" he cried.

Tessa said, "Exactly who are you practicing psychotherapy with?"

"First you. Then him." He beamed up at her from the floor.

"And what makes you think—"

"Blessings," he said, making a sign of the cross. "I retract every word. You are not pushy. You are merely turbulent." He called to me to fetch a bottle of Armagnac and again demanded that Tessa make a spoon. She curled up next to Quinn, who engulfed her in his huge arms. She closed her eyes and moved against him, laughing quietly. I stretched out on the couch and looked behind him into the dining room. Marty had vanished. The room was completely still now, the thick silence that follows any storm: the rain abates, the wind becomes a whisper. I stared at the ceiling, then craned my neck to look through the windows. It was snowing, pearl-gray snow; snow the color of oysters. I lay back against the pillows and closed my eyes. A rustle, someone replacing Bix with Brahms, the familiar Quartet in C minor, and the atmosphere cooled at once.

Marty settled sullenly on the floor, her back against my couch. Her mouth was set in a frown.

"Spoons," she muttered.

Yes?

"I thought he was talking about cocaine."

I smiled in the darkness.

"And that antique music."

Outside, it was snowing heavily. I thought that with luck we would be snowed in. Then I remembered Quinn's Land-Rover. No luck.

"And I hated Tessa's story."

The back of her head was only an inch or two from my face and her body was rigid, as if encased in armor. Her mailed arms were folded under her brass breasts, and she stared straight ahead. I had watched her while Tessa told her mother's story. Her eyes had clouded and she'd sat motionless. I knew she was committing it to memory, a cautionary tale. Now I took her hand and bent her head toward me. She didn't want to.

"Rich people," she said. "Wasted lives, like Quinn's."

I did not think of Quinn's life as wasted but I said nothing.

"Yellow cocktails," she said scornfully. "And the put-down of gay people. My soul mate in college was gay, and he was a very fine person. What you people can't stand. What you don't *get*. Is the demystification of sex." She went on in that way a moment, a charming tirade. I wondered why it was that I attracted angry women.

She said, "Are Quinn's books any good?"

"The last one was," I said. Her hand seemed to me as small and smooth as a child's. I heard Tessa purr and say something, but I avoided looking in her direction. I was thinking about Marty inside and out. She was a modern woman, come of age in the peace that followed the war. I tried to connect that with the demystification of sex, and couldn't. Perhaps they were not connected, or if they were she was correct and I didn't get it. Or couldn't stand it. She excited my imagination, and suddenly I thought of her as the mountain range west of my house, rising in seven different shades of blue, or as a nighttime snowfall, hushed but in irregular motion and obscure until you turned on the spotlights outside. Scheherazade.

I listened to Quinn's snore, then heard footsteps behind me, Tessa rising and leaving the room. Dispirited footsteps, I thought. Marty seemed suddenly to relax. I made room for her on the couch. We stared at each other a long moment, two strangers looking into the same mirror. Then she stretched out full length beside me. Her body softened at my touch. She pulled me close, continuing to smile in the darkness, her body moving against mine, the music all around us now.

◇

From the moment I saw her I wanted to fall in love with her. For me, sex was not demystified; I did not care that she was *sans merci*. The hat, the smile, the stillness, the suggestion of truculence, her freedom, her youth, her sarcasm, her dark rooms. And if I could make her love me back, so much the better. I thought I knew what was good for her. I had made so many mistakes, and been witness to so many others. . . .

Perhaps what I wanted most of all was revenge, for in my mind all this was vitally connected to my final, unwritten, somehow unwritable history of the Vietnam War, and the peace that followed.

six

She fell asleep at last, what looked like a deep and dreamless slumber, lying on her back. I curled up next to her and tried to sleep, but it was impossible. I touched her cheek and she stirred but did not waken. In repose her features did not change, though there was some softening around the mouth. The mouth enchanted me, it was sometimes a thin, pale line, it could use some softening. I lay on my side and looked at her in profile, her hair sprayed out on the white pillow. I burned her profile into my memory, in case she would decide to disappear; my emotions had raced so fast that my mind hadn't caught up and was suspended, loose somewhere.

Next morning, I was first up. The living room was dark. The low glass coffee table held a dish of starved flowers and an empty bottle of Armagnac, four ponies pulled up around it. Ashtrays overflowed and the sour odor of tobacco clung to the couch. I emptied the ashtrays and collected the empty bottle and the four ponies, brownly sticky with liquor. Then I opened the front door and stepped outside into a great white silence. I knew it would be there and had deliberately avoided looking out the windows or otherwise anticipating what I would find. It was the first snow, fresh, quiet, smooth, and without tracks. The small creatures were still burrowing out and the large ones floundering in the woods. The snow bowed the branches of the firs and lay thickly on the ground in a multitude of shapes, so lovely; there was no wind at all, the storm had blown itself out in the mountains. The air was cold but it was warm in the sun. I stood on Quinn's porch, squinting against the glare of the rising winter sun, listening to the near silence. Two huge icicles, hanging from the eaves, dripped sluggishly into the snowdrift beside the porch. The cars, Quinn's Land-Rover, Marty's Volkswagen, and my car, were covered; even the radio aerials sported little hats of snow. I guessed that about a foot had fallen and underneath it would be trouble; the skin of snow concealed treacherous ice. Straining, I listened for the rushing of the brook behind the house and in a moment it came, feebly, so feebly it might have been the racket of my own thoughts, my mind at last catching up with my emotions, echoing in my ears.

I stood motionless, watching. In the north country, a winter's morning after the first snowfall was always sacred, a kind of silent Te Deum in praise of miracles. We stood in awe of winter's enormity and surprise—snow pristine against a bright blue sky and the deep green of the maidenly firs, all bounded by mountains. We thought of it as the earth in its natural state. It brought to mind, often, cathedrals, as in a "cathedral silence." Standing on Quinn's porch, watching and listening, I decided that was the wrong image and the wrong religion. It was a civilized urban image and a religion devoted to iconography and to texts. When I thought of cathedrals I thought of Chartres or Burgos, great Gothic affairs smelling of incense and trembling with organ music, the stones reverberating from the music and the shuffling feet of communicants and tourists. There is nothing silent about a cathedral, whether it is crowded or not; it is noisy with its own bloody history, so ecstatic, contradictory, and conveniently explained. The church and its murderous crusades, its mystery, and its zeal; a priest's shoes, clattering along the marble, echo like a soldier's jackboots. Across

Quinn's lawn, a branch twitched and dumped a pillow of snow, then snapped back; a tiny bird flew off. I thought of a battered Christ, in agony on the cross, lit by the light of guttering candles while coins clinked in the collection box, all this in honor of or appeasement of or in supplication to a god who promised heaven in exchange for belief, and a confession of error. I hummed a hymn, Bunk Johnson's version of "Just a Closer Walk with Thee."

So much for cathedral silence. What did it have to do with a plain winter's morning in the north country, the morning of the first snow? No, it seemed to me that the first snowfall had the atmosphere of a Buddhist pagoda, silent, modest, concentrated. The snow was tao, covering things in their multitude of shapes, all white and benign. There was a concentration of sensation, and contradictions resolved exactly as I was warmed by the sun in the cold air. The north country resembled Kyoto more than Burgos. Buddhism did not exalt, it subsumed; it did not advance, it withdrew. I had known several Buddhist monks in the war and they were modest men, though political. Also, they were brave, often prepared to incinerate themselves for their beliefs. They were gnomic to interview, but they liked being interviewed; they all carried Sonys so they could tape me taping them. Once, in an effort to enter into the spirit of the transaction, I had my assistant tape them taping me taping them. I thought there was a koan there somewhere, though it would be useless in a news dispatch. At the end of my tour in the Zone I decided in my secular way that I admired Buddhism in the abstract, as a way of thinking rather than behaving, since the first five precepts for laymen forbid the taking of life, stealing, unchaste acts, false speaking, and the drinking of intoxicants. Or, I inferred from the discipline, tolerating those who did.

"You're muttering."

I turned around, it was Marty in her flannel pajamas, barefoot.

She kissed the tip of my nose. "What are you muttering about?"

I said, "My morning devotions."

She cupped her hands around a steaming cup of coffee, then offered some to me. She laughed, pointing. "Look there." She pointed to a spot in the snow, a little ripple the width of a pencil, moving. "A shrew," she said, "a little shrew heading for home, cute thing." Her bed-smell and the aroma of coffee was all around me. I put my arm around her waist and squeezed hard. She shivered and the shrew stopped moving. She said, "Look at that. I'll never get my car out. Do you suppose they plow Quinn's road?" Now she was frowning and I remembered her in bed, in repose; I had stared at her profile, expressionless in sleep, burning it into my memory because I was afraid she would disappear. She took a deep breath and exhaled, grinning suddenly. "Look at this day! This is the perfect day!" She moved languidly away from me, stretching, leaning over the porch railing, lifting her face to the sun. Little wisps of steam rose from her red flannel pajamas, still warm from bed, and I thought of her just then as a sexy bonze, in the instant following ignition. She cocked her head and laughed. "So what were you muttering about?"

I said, "Comparative religion."

"I took that in my freshman year and I was outstanding, just outstanding. The professor said so. He made a great effort to get me to come to dinner to discuss the Upanishads." She drained her coffee and shook the last few drops from the cup, little brown dots in the white snow.

"And soldier priests and political monks," I said.

She said, "You could get a dandy tan, in this sun."

"And unchaste acts," I said.

"So I have an idea." She turned to face me, her pajama top unbuttoned. There were goose bumps on her chest and the soft down on her belly flared. The drawstring of her pajamas had left a red mark on her belly. Her breasts were firm in the cold, her nipples hard against the flannel. The sun was at her back and seemed almost to create a nimbus around her head, her black hair mussed from sleep; her shadow was cast forward, her head touching my knees. She rubbed one foot against the other, then absent-mindedly buttoned the pajama top; I think she did not know it was open, and in any event the top button was missing. She was so trim and muscular, there wasn't a bit of fat anywhere. She said, "Let's take a cross-country ski, right here. Are you up for that? We'll take a lunch and put something hot in the thermos, it'll clear away the cobwebs. I'll call the mountain and tell them it's no dice today, I'm snowed in. Quinn and Tessa are still asleep and won't be awake for hours. How do you like that?" She put her arms straight out in front of her and touched her toes. Then she did a deep knee bend, holding for a count of ten, her body fixed and dead still. She looked up at me and winked. "How about that, darling?"

She padded back into the living room, leaving the door ajar. I watched her pause at the side table, pick up one of Quinn's week-old Boston *Globes*, and turn quickly to the comics page. She stared at it a full minute, concentrating fiercely; she stood in profile to me, tense, squinting, lips moving soundlessly. Suddenly she smiled and looked back at the side table, delicately pinching a pen from the letter tray. She scribbled for a moment, then tossed the paper aside and continued on her way. I stepped into the hall and looked at the paper. It was the Twistagram, done in a minute inside her head, the clues solved and assimilated.

PI

NIP

PAIN

PANIC

PACING

CAMPING

CAMPAIGN

An hour later we moved off up the road, side by side. She was using Tessa's skis and I was using Quinn's. We started slowly, working up a sweat, but after the first few hundred yards she waved good-bye and was gone, kicking and gliding, her arms pumping, the snow flying. Then she rounded the bend in the road and disappeared from view. When I reached the bend she was far ahead, out of sight, concealed now by trees.

I followed her tracks—there were no others—watching the trees as I skied. The trees seemed to move with me, confirming the view of modern physics that everything is in perpetual motion. The trail was uphill and I broke after thirty minutes, rested a bit, skied thirty more, and quit. Marty had taken the obvious route, up Quinn's road and through the forest following the old lumber trail. There was nothing special to see except trees—maple, birch, and fir. There were no animals about, only the occasional blackbird or hawk; even the grouse had gone to ground. I was sweating like a goat and my chest hurt.

I stopped where the trail breached the woods at the top of the rise. I stood listening to the silence, and soon I heard the *tap tap* of a woodpecker; it was the only sound. The land fell away to the west, and there was a grand panoramic view of pastureland and another high hill. The sun was directly overhead. I looked and saw Marty in the pasture, moving furiously. I watched her slow, then stop and turn around. She leaned on her poles a moment, her head drooping. She did an about-face in that strange penguin step skiers use, and began to retrace her route. I guessed she was about three miles away by the trail, perhaps half a mile as the crow flies. I watched her, moving slowly at first, then faster; I was trying to connect us. I saw myself at twenty-three, trying and trying to remember what it was that I thought and felt about things. But I could not get a purchase on that year, almost half my life away now. It was a struggle to remember whom I had worked for and where I had lived. I had no idea what I had believed in or if I had believed in anything; probably I had believed in journalism. I had kept a diary, really it was more a commonplace book, but it had been lost when I was away at the war, and now there was no way to revive those days except in the false light of what had come after; it was as if the loss of the journal had thrown a cloak over those years, and they had vanished except in the agreeably distorted mirror of the present. It was a mirror that could excuse but could not explain.

I unhooked my skis and stuck them in a snowbank, then shucked my backpack and unwrapped the lunch—soup, sandwiches, and fruit, cookies and coffee. I had packed a red tablecloth and spread that over a flat rock. Yellow granny apples looked pretty against the red tablecloth. They were bitter as hell, though. I thought, Aesthetics before utility; same as cathedrals. I wished I had brought a Heineken beer; the green bottles would be Christmasy next to the apples and the red tablecloth. I cut a fir bough instead and placed that at one end of the tablecloth. I looked at my handiwork and thought that I had missed my calling, just like Quinn. I could be maître 'd and he could be bartender. Quinn would never have forgotten the Heineken.

A movement caught my eye, and I looked up and saw Marty sprinting up the trail. I could hear her breathing, *unh-unh,* and the swish of her skis. Her eyes were on the trail and she was almost on me before she looked up and saw me. She gave a great heave and stopped pumping, gliding to a halt five feet away. Her face and hair were damp with sweat and her cheeks scarlet. She kicked off her skis and lay in the snow, arms flung out. She moved her arms and legs, angel's wings. Her breath exploded in gasps, then she was laughing and choking at once.

Oh, she said, *oh oh.* "That's so much fun, you know, to let it out like that. . . ." She was adjusting her sweatsuit, untying the drawstring. She had three layers of clothes on her upper body and was slick with sweat. "I was really up for it today, feeling light. Love to ski, *love* it. . . ." She made a wide sweeping motion with her hand, a bird on the wing.

I said, "You were flying."

"Yeah?" she asked, laughing again and tossing her head. Snow was melting where her head lay. "Lookin' good?" Then, frowning: "What happened to you?"

"I can't keep up with you," I said.

She said, "You've got to get in shape."

I said, "I am in shape."

"Better shape, then. I wasn't going particularly fast. Twice I stopped and almost went back along the trail, thinking that something had happened. I didn't know you weren't in shape. Well." She rose to one knee. "You've been busy, anyway. That's a nice spread. That's a good-looking picnic."

I said, "You were sexy, coming up the path."

"Yeah?" She looked at herself, then curiously at me. "How?"

"I don't know," I said. That was not quite the truth.

"We probably have different meanings for that word."

"I didn't know there was more than one," I said.

She said, "Neither did I."

In the little silence that followed, I pointed to the spread. Then I handed her an apple, which she took and polished against her thigh. We sat on a plastic blanket in the hot sun, not talking. She retied the drawstring of her sweatsuit. I unscrewed the thermos and poured coffee for us both. We were saving the sandwiches and soup. Marty stared into the middle distance, breathing easily now and chewing on her lower lip.

"It's probably the same definition," I said.

She said, "Whatever."

"Does it make a difference?" I thought we ought to get it behind us, whatever it was.

"It's strange, is all. We're skiing. Not anything else."

92

"Well," I said.

"And it got awfully heavy last night."

I picked up a sandwich, feeling her eyes on me. "That is not a news bulletin."

She said, "I didn't expect it."

"Life is full of surprises," I said cheerfully.

She was silent for a moment, then stood. She leaned against a bare maple, chewing thoughtfully on the apple. She said, "The first night, I didn't expect it. The mob in that house, so much confusion, I was late. We seemed to get it on so quickly, and it was such fun. It was a nice surprise. Then last night, I didn't expect that, either. And you weren't so cute and it wasn't so much fun."

I did not reply but thought to myself that we had different definitions for cute, too.

She said, "What do you want from me?"

I have never been good at answering direct questions. I prefer the carom shot, nuance kissing nuance. Now I looked west, to the pasture below and the mountain in the distance. I was making another effort to see myself at twenty-three, ambitious and unencumbered. This was about as easy as transmogrifying oneself into a bear in order to hibernate for a season, or to participate in the life of the den.

"We don't have to force it," I said.

"I'm supposed to be the careful one?"

"Right," I said.

"Me?"

"You."

"That's not my metabolism," she said, shaking her head and pitching the apple into the woods.

"I've fallen for you," I said, clearing my throat. "I've fallen in love with you." It was what I had told her the night before, more than once, as if by repetition we could both become accustomed to the fact and it would be neither surprising nor extraordinary, merely a fact like any other. "I don't know what to do about it," I confessed. "But it's the truth." Looking at her leaning against the maple, I decided that she looked older than her years; she was plenty old enough, anyhow.

She raised her leg, arching her foot, then lowered it slowly to the snow.

"So here we are," I said.

She paid no attention, lost in some memory of her own.

"I didn't expect it, either," I said. I touched her hand but she did not move. Her hand was warm but inert.

All right, Marty said grimly. She would relate some history of her own. You don't know anything about us, she said. She was from a different milieu, one I had no contact with and no understanding of. She said, We are not exclusive. We don't take blood oaths and we don't expect so much. She'd received a letter the other day from her old lover. She'd replied to it right away. It was friendly and quite funny, not at all what she'd feared when she saw the familiar handwriting under the strange postmark. He wanted to come up to see her and she'd said, Come ahead; come anytime. They were friends now, and they both knew that getting into a relationship again would be like rerunning a race. The meet was over and the times recorded and nothing had changed in the meantime. Like, it was an episode, part of the past and she was eager to get on into the future. They both were, but it did not mean they could not be friends and affectionate with each other. She was through with love affairs for a while. She did not want to go through it again with him or any man, just then. And she was no longer in love with him; she had been, and God knows had proved it in a dozen different ways. But she'd allowed herself to be manhandled and even now, looking back on it, she was not entirely certain why. She had had a theory then that you had to follow everything through to the last inch. If it was valuable enough to do at all, it was valuable enough to do thoroughly; no loose ends, and no exhaustion. So they'd split and reunited and split and reunited and split again and reunited again until she felt like a sail with no control over the wind. He was the wind, and she intended no pun; he was the most intelligent and inventive man she'd ever known and a nonstop talker; listening to him for an evening was a postgraduate education. *That* was sexy, and the one thing she knew was that they'd be friends forever. He'd read everything and what he hadn't read he could fake. Not a man troubled by bourgeois ambition, he knew exactly where the world was and where it was going, and he intended, as he said, to bleed on the leading edge. And of course he insisted that she bleed with him, casualties together in the long struggle for . . . justice. Coruscating together, they would be entitled to claim the victory, for Marx and the new physics—ecstasy, rapture without limit. No limits anywhere along the line.

She looked at me sourly. Wasn't it interesting about men? They were never more adorable than when on a high wire, full of piss and vinegar, in motion, moving on. They just swept you along, delighted that you'd hold your breath with the rest of the audience. "There's something about them then, almost—"

"Chivalrous?" I suggested.

"No," she said. Then, "Shelby was a space shot." For her old lover, the most beautiful words in the language were *absolutely, Shelby, whatever you say.* She shared his bed and his ideals but was not prepared, did not feel obligated, to share every opinion, political, economic, social, and literary. He was filled with opinions, obsessed as he was by the shape of things to come. But he'd been an education, not least into the anatomy of the male ego, fragile as an eggshell when it was not strong as pigiron. And he was a man who had his share of demons. She'd loved him and understood him and thought for a while that he was her way into herself, that he and his prodigious energies could inspire a leap of the imagination. . . . But there was no room for her. For a while that didn't matter; while she was holding her breath it didn't matter. Then it did. She felt she had to insist, or become invisible, a face in the crowd. So things came apart, and at the end they were definitely not cool together. The demons won and they were entitled to the victory. No, that was not true. They had simply won and whether they were entitled to win was something else.

Living with him, she said, was like living with a . . . little Quinn! A younger, more whimsical, more passionate, radical Quinn. A Quinn without a tangled history. A young lord of misrule, that was Shelby, ideals intact even if scattered. A Quinn with a social conscience, a combination of young Verkovensky and old Karamazov—though there was nothing European about Shelby, he was American through and through, a loyal son of blue-collar West Allis, a dumb ox of a town. His values were admirable and it was fun, Jesus he was fun, my space shot, living always inside his locomotive. Moving on.

She was silent a moment, then laughed loudly. I leaned forward, it was the first full-throated laugh I'd heard. She sat up, legs crossed Indian-fashion, bubbling with laughter.

"Do you know what he did once? In college, he lived down the hall from me. Owned a Volkswagen bus, an old broken-down bus, blue. One day he was walking to the dining hall and stopped at a corner where a school bus was letting off some kids. He watched the driver work the lever that opened the door, and that reminded him of his own grade-school days, very happy days for him. Shelby had a happy childhood, as I did. He thought it would be superb if he could build the identical apparatus to work the door of his bus, the VW. In that way he'd be reminded always of his own happy school days in West Allis, Wisconsin. With anybody else it would've ended there, a neat idea, unconsummated. Not Shelby. He worked on it for two months, did nothing else. And he *did* it, built the fucker, and the sliding door of the VW worked just like the old yellow school bus in West Allis.

"At about the same time he discovered—he was late coming to some things—that dope had certain properties he liked. Now this was an old VW, imported from Germany naturally, and had a little flower pot attached to the front dashboard. He replaced the dead peonies with grass, right? But he found he'd forget to water the plants and of course they'd die, just like the peonies. Anybody else—well, anybody else wouldn't've tried to grow dope in a Volkswagen, and if they did would've arranged to keep a watering can handy. Not Shelby. He knew right away what to do, how to water his plants at the touch of a fingertip. Think about it a minute, it's obvious, like all great inventions." I shook my head, mystified; it was not obvious to me. "He rewired the windshield washer so it came around inside the car. Presto! An automatic sprinkler! A major garden!" Marty laughed again, throwing her head back. "Gee," she said, "he was something, Shelby. Then he discovered politics as he had discovered dope and decided that politics was even more hallucinogenic, a proposition I agreed with in the beginning. Except it went on too long. Essentially he's an inventor. He's Benjamin Franklin but he thinks he's Thomas Paine." She rocked forward, hugging her knees. She was sweating, giving off a thick, musty smell. "My sexy friend Shelby, I miss him. . . ." The stories had come in a rush, relived as they were retold, and were a part of her in a way that I could never be. Describing Shelby, Marty was the happiest I'd ever seen her. "So," she said, serious again, pausing to pour coffee, "there's that." There was a sudden chill as the clouds from the west finally overtook the sun. I had been watching them, a heavy gray line advancing toward us; it looked as if there would be more snow. We moved closer together, two motionless people surrounded by snow in its multitude of shapes, and the silence of the country.

She was up suddenly and stepping into her skis. One sprint, she said, then we could head back. She positioned herself on the trail, then pushed off in the abandoned motion, arms and legs levering, that racers use. The smell of her clung to the snow. I watched her go, moving easily now, her head forward. I heard an odd noise and realized she was laughing. What was it? A memory of Shelby no doubt, some amusing or unusual sexual encounter; no doubt he was as clever with love as he was with mechanics. But he had manhandled her; she said they were not suited. It sounded as if he had a mine field of his own, perhaps more than one. Their love affair would have reached its climax at about the time of the fall of Saigon, the end of one nightmare and the beginning of another; I wondered if they had followed the news in Madison. Perhaps they had watched the news nonstop as I had, though they would have rooted for Nicholson; they would have wished disgrace to my friend the diplomat. Nicholson had told me that after he returned to Washington he found a bag full of mail, almost five hundred letters; many of them were from students. They had loved his work and wanted to know how to become a war correspondent. The majority of the letters were from young women who sent photographs of themselves. They were good-looking young women, Nicholson said. He found himself a favorite on campuses and took a month off to lecture. *My God,* he'd said, *I'm a hero. They think I'm Ed Murrow. And the fees!* I wondered if Marty and Shelby had watched him, after watering the plants. Having put the American experiment to rights, they'd make love. Again and again and again, the old bus rocking like a dinghy at anchor and inside the stink of grass.

She was gone now, invisible in the forest, and her scent dissolved, driven away by the cold and the light breeze that had come up. I collected the remains of our picnic, trying to imagine life at a university in the year 1975. It would have been a disappointing year for anyone who craved action. The gains of the decade before were secure, the lightning breakout of the seventh decade of the century overturning the known world in what seemed like the twinkling of an eye—or perhaps it was only a lewd wink— the wood so rotten it crumbled to sawdust at the slightest touch. 1975: indubitably a transitional year, though ripe with confirmation, failure following failure—military defeat, political scandal, capitalism itself creaking and groaning, struggling in a tide of red ink.

I imagined them laughing, playing with each other, watching the ruined ambassador on television. Shelby's place, his book-filled apartment in a down-at-heel neighborhood near the campus, an old poster of Huey Newton *avec fusil* on the wall over the battered black-and-white with a wire coat hanger for an antenna. They would not know the ambassador's name, only that he was the last defeated proconsul, his eyes hidden by dark aviator's glasses, clutching his leather briefcase filled with the cyphers and the EYES ONLY/ NO DIS cables. *No comment*, he said again and again; then, at last, to a reporter who seemed friendly, or anyway less marauding, a muttered, bitter epitaph. Or that was what it sounded like, over the noise. Perhaps it was an oath or prayer. It was certainly not an apology. He looked to be near tears, his voice so heavy with weariness and depression, of the certain knowledge that this was the last and most terrible scene of the ghastly drama. The corpses now littered the stage, and all that was left was for the curtain to fall, and for him to return to his capital and appear before the appropriate committees of Congress.

Dead piled on dead, a hecatomb. They would turn to each other, burning with desire, and the story would go on and on unwatched; film of the evacuation, pretty young correspondents in jungle fatigues reporting from the decks of aircraft carriers. Helicopters landing, disgorging their cargoes, then dumped over the side. A Huey was a two-million-dollar aircraft. I had grown up with all that, from the moment the parlor in my grandfather's house had gone silent and we heard the first staccato dispatches from New York that Pearl Harbor had been attacked. There had been that, the bomb, and then the end of that; and then Korea and the end of that; and McCarthy and Eisenhower, Hiss, the Hungarian Revolution, the U-2, Kennedy's election, and then the end of Kennedy. And hovering over all of it, like some ghost from the edge of the continent where everything swung free, a dark vapor always with us in good times and bad, Nixon. I wanted clear vision, a salient moral sight, but my memory was too cluttered. The rooms were crowded with people, and that familiar figure everywhere I looked. His shadow was as long and large as Lincoln's, he colored everything, every day, every hour, from the end of the Second World War.

I began to laugh, conjuring an ageless, unshaven Nixon as Count Dracula, poised in the pasture below, spreading his bat-arms, fingers spastic in the V sign, Churchill's sign, his eerie shadow lengthening, the white snow stained dark. His shadow would never reach Ms. Neher, however; however long it got, it would never get quite long enough. Nixon was no threat, he meant no more to her than Jim Morrison did to me. They were both messengers of cultural infantilism, the signal of collapse as surely as any disintegrating keystone or clubfooted Mercury. Of course this was not to say that they did not possess a certain aggressive, malignant genius. A certain comfortable purchase on our disordered national will. They went to the heart of things, give them that; their beat was strong, the little devils.

"Why are you laughing?" She was in front of me, leaning on her skis, bending at the waist, gulping great drafts of air. She looked adorable.

"I could tell you," I said, "but it would be wrong." I laughed again, but she didn't get the reference. "I could take the easy way. . . ."

She reached inside her shirt and unhooked her bra.

I said, "I was thinking about Nixon and what a national treasure he was—is!—and how sad it is that you never knew him in his salad days." She grunted, one of the hooks was caught. I realized suddenly that Nixon was the generational link, my father's generation, my generation, hers. I had no doubt that he would last the century, my grandchildren could watch him on *Meet the Press*, an antique like Carmine de Sapio or Buffalo Bill. I said, "When you were at Madison with Shelby, did you have a television set?" She nodded, distracted, still struggling with the hook. "And did you watch the fall of Saigon on the television set?"

"No," she said. Then, "This thing is caught."

"You didn't watch the fall?"

"Of course not," she said.

"Why not?" I asked.

"I don't remember. What was the point?" She said, "Will you do me?" She put her back to me. She was breathing heavily. Her skin was slick and hot in the cold air. Her musty odor was all around us. I took off my gloves and worked to unhook the bra, then slid my hands around and cupped her breasts. I leaned into her and kissed the back of her neck, where her hair was wet. I felt her nipples stiffen under my fingers, her breasts heavy and slippery as soap. . . .

"That's nice," she said, "but not now." She moved her shoulders, irritated, and turned to face me. "You've got to learn. It's the same at night, out goes the light and—bang bang—you're on top of me, regardless. And now, same thing."

I was going to explain that it was the way many of us chose to express affection. A clever enough retort, and true as far as it went. But there was something else. Thinking about the war and about Nixon, and inevitably about my own life in that dark time, I had wanted to draw close and hold her.

"You make it such a big deal," she said.

"Yes," I admitted.

"And it isn't." She looked away west, at the mountain and the clouds moving over it. "I like it when we talk. When it's light and we're equals . . ." She smiled suddenly. "As a matter of fact, what I remember most about that year was watching reruns of *Leave It to Beaver*." She laughed. Shelby thought it was a metaphor, capitalist propaganda. He thought it was written by someone at the Republican National Committee, but there were darker implications than that, sexual implications. That family, Mom, Dad, Wally, the Beav . . ." She went on to explain the sexual implications. I listened

101

hard but I had trouble following her because I had never seen *Leave It to Beaver*. Whatever it was, sitcom or cartoon, I could not get it on my single channel. Yet the story was funny and I laughed appreciatively. "For his English class, Shelby wrote Beaver scripts as Ibsen might or Odets or Herbert Marcuse. . . ."

"Pinter," I said.

She reached down to pick up the coffee and drain it. She turned away from me, her eyes inward; she seemed to concentrate, and then she put her hand on my arm. It was a gesture of complicity and affection, almost sisterly in its understanding. She said softly, "I know you need me."

I stepped back, astonished; no woman had ever said that to me. I said, "I do." Then, to break the dense silence that followed, I laughed. She looked at me, smiling. I pointed down at the pasture. A lone skier was breaking ground, his track parallel to hers. It began to flurry, hard little flakes. The skier was dressed in fluorescent orange, frightened no doubt of the deer hunters. The snow came down. We watched the skier as he crossed the pasture into the forest and was lost to view.

seven

There was more snow that afternoon and evening, but early the next morning the town's snowplow dug us out, so Marty went to work. Tessa took the Land-Rover to drive to St. J. for provisions. Quinn was working downstairs in his study, typing furiously. I stoked the fire and settled on the couch with the *Guardian*, which Quinn received each day by mail. The *Guardian* carried a long report on the boat people of Indochina; I read it carefully, each word.

Hundreds of boats, thousands of people, more every day, all far from home. Boats blown by the trade winds to all the great ports of South Asia, Singapore and Hong Kong and Manila, various locations on the Malay Penninsula. The authorities did not know what to do with the people. Many boats swamped and those that arrived were filled with sick and injured. Stoic faces, the report said, undernourished but content enough to survive the sea, pleased to be anywhere but in their homeland. One more legacy from our brave little war, I thought; human beings scattered like driftwood throughout Asia, washing up now on this beach, now on that. I thought that for the rest of our lifetimes, wherever we go, we will find Vietnamese. No corner of the earth will be too remote. We will find them in Asia, in Europe, in Latin America, in Africa and Australia, and in towns along the Mississippi. Asian children will grow up learning to spell M-i-s-s-i-s-s-i-p-p-i. There will be a literature and in time a Vietnamese Mark Twain, a Twain to celebrate the necessity of lighting out for the territory. Ho Chi Minh as Aunt Sally, the United States as the great river itself, vast and indifferent. Come back to the raft ag'n, Nguyen. There will be communities of them everywhere on this earth, like Jews, assimilated but always standing slightly apart, always slightly suspect, and therefore always and especially—apprehensive. I put the paper down and stared into the fire. I put another log on the fire, thinking that probably there were Vietnamese in St. J. And if there were, did they have a pagoda?

I heard a noise behind me and suddenly Quinn was in the room, bearing a pot of hot coffee and sandwiches. He was taking a break, having worked since seven that morning. It had been an excellent day for him because there were no women to interfere with his concentration.

He said, "Tell me about Carla."

"She's fine," I said. "Says she is, anyway." I was having trouble bringing myself back from the boat people, Mark Twain and the Mississippi, and the rest of it.

"Did the girl get into Foxcroft?"

I turned away, embarrassed. I hadn't thought to ask. Foxcroft was very distant. "I think so," I said.

"Did you ask specifically?"

"No," I confessed. "I forgot about the girl."

"It's important to her," Quinn said. "Where the child goes to school. It makes a difference. She's a very bright child, deserves the best. Carla wants her to have a career and you can't begin the groundwork too early. Foxcroft is first-rate, Tessa's mother went to Foxcroft. A number of very prominent women have gone to Foxcroft. I wish to Christ you'd asked." He lit a cigarette, exhaling in a rush. "What about him?"

"Nick?" I smiled. "He goes from success to success."

Quinn nodded, unconvinced.

"Only guy I know who went from the box to print, instead of the other way around. Of course his background's print, you remember the thing he did on Ché Guevara. But the column's going well. Carla says he has a hundred papers, which is good after only one year. No one thought he could do it."

"He was a world-class interviewer," Quinn said. "Best interviewer I ever saw; when Vietnam was going down the drain the BBC used to pick up his stuff. But that's all he could do, interrogate. He couldn't think worth shit."

"That's the feature of the column," I said. "That's what he promises them, an exclusive interview a week. Three columns a week, one of them's an interview. That's his edge."

Quinn grunted. "I suppose he gives them a deputy assistant to the deputy assistant."

I smiled. "Sometimes not even."

"Well," Quinn said. "Any messages?"

"She sends her best." That was an utterly accurate answer to his question. When I had spoken to Carla the week before, she had said, "Give Quinn my best, when you see him."

"What the hell," he said. "You can't blame her. It's only two years they've been married."

I did not reply to that.

"He's steady anyway. That's what you need, the second time around. Steadiness."

I laughed. "He's an alcoholic."

"No," Quinn said thoughtfully. "He's a drunk. An alcoholic is someone who goes to meetings."

I laughed again. "He has a drinking problem."

"Wrong again," Quinn said grimly. "He's a problem drinker. You and I, we have drinking problems."

"What's the difference?"

"He's an asshole and we're not."

"No, he's a good guy."

"That's what Carla thinks. That's why she married him."

"He's good to her kid."

"Christ," Quinn said. "How long does that last?"

"It never ends," I said. "The kid's always there, and as long as he's good to her Carla'll be there too. She's seen too many of her friends marry a second time for love and have it not work out. She's very practical, Carla. And Nick's all right."

"It makes me sick," Quinn said.

"I like Tessa," I said.

"She thought the kid couldn't fit into my life and I suppose she was right, I don't have a lot of spare room. But aren't they supposed to go away at a certain age? To school and then to university? And aren't they supposed to see their father on vacation? And aren't they supposed to get married? Are they around forever?"

"Forever and a day," I said, smiling.

"What the hell ever happened to American ingenuity?" Quinn rose and shuffled to the window and peered out, as if he would find the old get-up-and-go in the woods white with snow. "Leaving the nest, going west for fame and fortune, et cetera." He looked at me belligerently, and I thought for a moment that all this was a prelude to one of his lectures on American cultural history. "What the hell, are they around all the time now?"

"They're children, Quinn. If you have children, the children're around. It's called family."

"The English have the right idea. They hate their children."

"They send them away when they're six," I said.

"She said I wasn't made for marriage. I was not the type to be a married man. Not *suitable,* she said."

"I know," I said. "I think you've mentioned that before."

"*Au contraire,* I told her. I'd make a fine father given half a chance." He turned again to the window. "She acts as if when you get married you're not supposed to have any more fun."

"You have too many friends," I said.

106

"Or friends, either."

"And your trips, researching the books."

"That's my livelihood," he said, "and it's inviolate. I'll tell you something. She's the best editor I ever saw. Knows what's in your mind before you do. Understands narrative. Has perfect taste. Can see into your soul, that miserable thicket. Every man should have one, editor like that. You should." He sat down again, weary. "But why did she have to marry that asshole?"

"Nick's all right."

"I don't mean Nicholson, that hack. I mean the other one. The first one, the girl's father. *That* one."

I sighed. We had had this conversation many times, but Quinn never tired of it. To him it had as many facets as a diamond; and like a diamond, it blinded him. He hated both of Carla's husbands and often confused them in his mind. I said, "She was twenty-one and wanted to get out of the house and there was only one respectable way to do it. Why do you suppose we all got married at twenty-one and had children as if they were cocktails?" That was true, but it was also true that we were bewitched by romance and strung as tight as piano wire with sexual tension. And we wanted the responsibility, *craved* it, responsibility being the prerequisite for manhood. Also, and not incidentally, America was a paradise for children. A baby carriage: the only convertible that outsold Ford. Of course Quinn saw responsibility in a different light. He had never married, never would marry; no regrets. I said, "Then she left him and you came along, or I guess it was the reverse because she left him for you. But he was still there because he was the first." And because he represented so much, I thought but did not say; in America, a first love was indelible. It was the first story of which you were indisputably the hero, or the author. Or one of the authors, every personal story having more than one author of it. "And he was the father of the girl and so forth and so on, and for that reason he'll always be there, one way and another. She had a long time alone and now she's happy or says she is. And she sends her best. And if it's Nicholson, so what?"

Quinn wasn't listening. "It would've been fine if she'd *stuck*. Remember that last picnic we had, with the Fortnum's hamper and the rest of it? The champagne. It was in Hyde Park, near the Serpentine. A troop of Horse Guards cantered by. That was our great chance, that time. We could've started off fresh together. Then she went back after we'd quarreled—and it would be nice if I could say that I don't remember what the quarrel was about but I do, every detail—and then we got together again but it wasn't the same. The next quarrel was worse and the next was worse still. I know what it was, she wanted somebody else. I mean, she wanted me all right but me made over. I did not conform to the image she had of me. I was like a political candidate who's presented as one thing and turns out to be another. Like Muskie crying. And part of that was her first husband. And now, to think of her with *Nicholson*. That hack."

"Watched him every day of the week, when Saigon fell. That was before he had the column, he was playing cat and mouse with a friend of mine. He's damn good on the box."

"I'll bet he is," Quinn said. "He's damned good on the box and damn good with her girl. And he's a hack."

"What the hell," I said. "She's happy."

"No, she isn't," Quinn said. "She's not miserable. She makes do. It's enough for her, maybe, but not enough for me, by God."

"Well," I said.

"I wish to God you'd asked about the girl. I used to call her, late at night after I'd had twenty-five cocktails. But I haven't done that in a while." He sat quietly a moment, brooding. "Tessa's all right," he said. "But she's got to let up on me and I don't think she's going to. She's got some kind of crazy image, too. She's too much like her mother, they all are. Damn good piece of advice my ma gave me once. Look at a girl's mother because that's what she'll become. So that means some turbulence, if the mother's a loony. And you've fallen for Marty and that's a laugh. What's got into you anyway?"

I looked at him. "A helicopter."

"Friendly or enemy?"

I explained about the helicopter flying over my house, the banker inspecting building sites. Condominiums spoiling the wilderness of the north country. People replacing bears. Then I explained about the ship in the bottle. While I was about it, I added several relevant details of my isolated life in New England.

"And you can't finish your book."

"That, too," I said. "That's the ship in the bottle."

"And you think Marty's the answer to that."

"You said it, Quinn. Every man needs an editor." I added, "I don't like the life I had and thought I'd borrow a new one for a while."

"Mine," he said cheerfully.

I laughed and decided to tell Quinn about the decoy sheep. This was a favorite story of my father's. He believed the decoy sheep to be the salient metaphor of American ingenuity, resilience, pragmatism, and virtue. In the old days in the Chicago stockyards a decoy sheep was introduced into a pen of sheep destined for the knife. The decoy sheep was trained to conduct its comrades to the killing pen, a majordomo to the abattoir. But as the herd collected around the gate the decoy sheep, first in line, began inconspicuously to drop back. The herd went north as the decoy sheep went south, walking backward (according to my father). When the decoy sheep was alone in the holding pen it was returned to the yards to do it all over again the next day. In that way the decoy sheep lived to a happy old age. My father told this story with humor and perspective.

Quinn looked at me strangely and grunted.

I said, "You can look it up. It's in Dreiser somewhere, that story."

He said, "I'm sure."

"You're lucky to have Plumb," I said. What a convenience, I thought, to create a hero; it solved so many problems, and there would never be a conflict of interest.

He said, "*Au contraire.* Plumb is lucky to have me." He hesitated a moment. "I don't know why you ever came up here to live. It was a bum idea."

"I wanted to get away from the war," I said. "I thought the way into the war was looking at it from afar. But it wasn't, and that last chapter's a bastard. The trouble isn't distance, it's intimacy. I've got to get up close again and see every pore. Listen to it. Smell it." I thought about the high hopes, leaving for the north country. "And things could've turned out differently."

"If you were different," Quinn said. "But you're not. You're a bourgeois, same's me. That's what we are, though sometimes we like to think we're bohemians, and that's where we screw up. Europeans understand that you bear the weight of your childhood and your parents and their parents and where you were born and grew up—your whole history— and it's immutable, like blue eyes and a bald head. Try to change any of it and all you do is thrash around and make trouble, and then there's instability and you don't win, you lose. You're up a creek without a paddle."

I smiled. "Whatever you say."

He said, "Let's have a beer."

When he returned with the beer, I said, "What do you think of her?"

"She's a friend of mine," Quinn said.

"I know that," I said.

"She's adorable, she's very young and impressionable. She's younger than Springtime. And Tessa says she's scared."

"Of *me?*"

"Of what you might do."

I smiled widely. "She's not stupid."

Quinn drank, a long draft. He said quietly, "She says you carry around too much baggage, ness pa? And she thinks you want to give it to her and she doesn't fancy

110

herself a redcap, no suh." He looked at me and grinned wolfishly, the beer held steady under his nose. He said it was his considered opinion that I back off and think a little; as I well knew, in matters of the heart he was almost never wrong. A question of the baggage, so much of it. He went on to describe the particular pieces, the portmanteaus, the two-suiters, and the briefcases; all of them had cracked leather and were slightly damaged, as they had been in use for upwards of forty years. He was enjoying himself hugely, and I suspected that he was trying out an idea for a book, "Plumb's Baggage." I could see the dust jacket in my mind's eye, and it wasn't a bad title. His left hand tapped out a little riff on the coffee table. I half listened to him, nodding when it seemed the thing to do, frowning otherwise. I was think-ing about my own book, untitled; untitled, unfinished, its author undone. Unlike Quinn, so surefooted and confident.

Watching him, I remembered another occasion many years before. It was a pub lunch that had begun at noon and ended hours later in his flat in South Kensington. He was still working at the bank, wanting to write but not knowing what to write; Plumb had not yet arrived. Carla had gone back to America, to try to make it up with the father of her daughter. I remembered Quinn that night at the white piano, very drunk but playing wonderfully. He had described the various ways in which his life was over, "*finito.*" He said, "I'll be glad when you're dead, you rascal, you." I remembered him looking at me wearily, his fingers moving so slowly over the keys. He said, "I think I'd rather play them than listen to them. Twelve bars, three-line stan-zas. The third and the seventh of the key are fundamental, and of course they're flatted. Those are the blue notes." He played a moment in silence and then went on, distracted, as if talking to himself. He said his blues were a strict form, like a sonnet, and you had to know the structure. He raised his hands in front of his face and smiled at me through his fingers. "Those bars are made of iron, the American blues." He said, "The theme is announced in the first four bars.

Then it's repeated, with variations. First four bars are straight, second four aren't. The theme is answered in the final four, which are all blue. Those final four bars are instructive, like the couplet ending a sonnet. That's the consolation, when there is any." I thought of that now, as his fingers tapped the coffee table. Within the form everything was improvised, always pushing, always ambitious. There was freedom so long as you stayed inside the form, obeying its laws; it was remarkably spacious, though its limits were fixed. Revels in a penitentiary.

Later still, standing at the window—it was a balmy summer night and the window was thrown open to the street—Quinn had said he knew, he simply *knew*, that this was the lowest point his life would ever reach. He was far from home but he had made his own choice and would stick with it. He would be an exile, disengaged; and he would do something conspicuous. He was not meant to live in the background. Carla had no confidence, that was the trouble. She was not prepared to *risk*. Perhaps it was just as well, probably he was a solo character. And that meant he had to look out for himself. Wasn't that what the blues taught? You had to defend your own life. Every man had to be a patriot in his own country, and ready and willing to take up arms at a moment's notice because there were barbarians everywhere, poised for invasion. They wanted to take it from you, whatever it was. Invasion parties were always over the next hill. Living in that screwed-up country, she didn't know what she wanted. There was so much of everything, and the supply was inexhaustible. She knew what she was supposed to want, but that wasn't the same thing. She's not a high-wire man, he said. That's the point, I am. Always will be, or anyway will be as long as I have the balance for it. Then Quinn began to talk faster and faster, still looking out the window into the warm English night. He talked about Carla, how they'd met and where, and what she meant to him. Then he talked about his unwritten books, the characters he intended to explore;

112

there were so many of them. He would define his territory in his books. And as for Carla: there wouldn't be anyone else, ever.

I did not take that declaration seriously—an error, as it turned out.

He'd said, "If you allow just anyone to walk in and take part of your country, annex a province, seize a port city, impose taxes and laws, why then, you've forfeited . . ." He didn't finish this fantastic thought, or if he did I didn't hear it; he was talking to the silent street. I was listening carefully, too, trying to connect it all to my own life, so solid then, so secure. But I was not a high-wire man, nor was my wife. I did not think of myself as besieged, a nation surrounded by enemies. I was surprised by his passion and moved by the light in which he cast himself; he seemed to see the world as a stage or narrative. It was obvious that night that one part of his life was truly over and another about to begin. I wondered if he had the courage to quit the bank.

Suddenly he stopped talking and wheeled on me, his face livid, skin stretched tight across his bones. He crouched wide-eyed, pounding his fist into his palm. He said he had a compulsion to fix things, put them right. Advise, counsel, guide; that was what he wanted to do in his books, pose complicated problems and then solve them. That was the way he would live, altering experience, distilling memory, arranging the universe to suit himself, no explanations necessary. Or apologies, either. His history, his story. A life was *not* a narrative, that was the trouble with it. He would draw the truth from the disorder around him—what else was there?—and everything was material, every single thing. And naturally he would stay ahead of the times, working always into the future, invaluably sided by the solitariness, the sovereignty, the oneness, of his own life.

Hadn't he neglected one thing? My constant companion in my own frequent journeys into solipsism: "And your guilt," I said.

113

He raised his eyes and looked at me coldly. "I am not a religious man."

I didn't know what that had to do with it and said so.

He said, "Guilt is a distraction, a waste of time and energy and therefore an offense against nature."

"But not against God," I said. It was a question.

He said, "I don't know anything about God. Or about guilt. That's your department. But my conscience is my own." It was the only time we ever talked about God and it made us both uncomfortable. Neither of us said anything for a moment. Finally I asked him where Carla fit in.

The hell with that, he said at last. I have the memory of her and I don't need anything else. I have a hell of a good memory and that's the one thing they can never take away from you. Some people need guilt, it keeps them going; it makes them ambitious. I don't need it.

All that was close to twenty years ago. He had had a fine passage, from the bed-sitter in South Kensington to Chester Square and his American office. He had his houses and his books and seemed to have kept his promises to himself along with his independence, so prized. No one had a claim on him; he was guilt-free, solo.

"It seemed like such a good idea," I said suddenly.

"Well, it wasn't," Quinn said. "It was my idea, too. I thought you'd be good for each other."

"I don't mean her," I said. "I mean the north country. Maybe we don't have a taste for frontiers any more. I don't know how they did it, the early settlers. Cold, hard ground. No spring and a short summer. Dangerous, all you have to do is look at the cemeteries: women dying in childbirth, children a few years later. And lonely beyond imagining."

He said, "A lot of people like it."

"They do for a while," I said. "Then they leave, because the truth is, the land's exhausted. The people are. Even the damned weather. *That's* exhausted."

"Marty—" he said tentatively.

"Is not exhausted," I said. Then, "It's a patriotic duty,

chasing after her. I'm the only thing that stands between her and the childhood lover. I'm the last line of defense. Did you know she had a boyfriend who grew dope in a flowerpot that hung on the dashboard of a Volkswagen bus?" Quinn began to laugh. "Wired the windshield washer so it'd sprinkle his plants and he'd have dope the year round, winter and summer, rain or shine or snow. Something of a political philosopher as well, this lad. And a hard case who specialized in Ed Gein country, up near Sheboygan." Quinn was roaring now. He had named Plumb's editor, Ed Gein, after the Wisconsin cannibal of the fifties who was Hitchcock's inspiration for *Psycho*. I said, "From him to me, don't you think that's a leap of the imagination? I'm going to be to Marty Neher what the British Museum was to Marx."

"What's she going to be to you?"

"Warm Springs," I said. I was looking over Quinn's shoulder at a photograph, my wife and me at a restaurant in Paris following a long raucous lunch. Quinn had taken the picture, such a cheerful shot, crumpled napkins and empty wine bottles and my wife smiling her familiar lopsided smile. My mouth was open, the beginning of a laugh; Quinn had said something funny. That had been a three-hour lunch at a restaurant near Les Halles. How many years ago? Perhaps ten. My wife had a fine, distinctive smile, recognizable even in her baby pictures. In the lower right-hand corner of the photograph was a full snifter of something, probably marc de bourgogne, slender fingers touching its base. Quinn's girl. I couldn't remember who she was, but she had a good-looking hand, something in the way her nails touched the glass indicated impatience. No wonder, she was doubtless bored to distraction. I remembered that we had had tickets for the opera that night, and we arrived tipsy and disheveled, Quinn talking loudly in his execrable French.

He saw me looking at the photograph and said, "Your wife puts up with a hell of a lot."

I nodded. That was true enough.

"And now," he said, "*here,* to hell and gone. Even three months is too much for me, I can't imagine it the year-round."

The conversation was moving in an unhappy direction. I said, "The only thing I like about it is the clothes. I like flannel shirts and corduroys and heavy shoes. I once went a year without wearing a tie. You have no idea how much you can save on dry cleaning, Quinn."

"That's how you spend your evenings then, you two. Reading the Bean's."

"Not only Bean's," I said. "There're Orvis catalogs and Eddie Bauer and Eastern Mountain Sports and about half a dozen others. More fun than F.A.O. Schwarz when you were a kid."

"Uh-huh," he said.

"And of course it's not just looking, it's buying, too. It's a red-letter day when the mailman comes with the package from Bean's or Bauer's. Once I bought an inflatable rubber boat from Bean's; that was a pretty special day."

"I'll bet it was," Quinn said.

I pointed at the picture. "Who was she, your date at lunch? I can't remember her name."

"I don't know what her name is," Quinn said.

I said, "Remember the opera? We were so tight. I think it was *Così fan tutte.* . . ."

He said, "Is this what she wanted, when she started out? When you started out together, what were her expectations? When you thought about the future, what did you think about? What was the shape of things? I mean, in terms of what you wanted from life. Is this what she thought she'd be, a mom in the mountains to the back of beyond? The year-round, winter and summer and everything in between? Or do you think she wanted something else?"

"Quinn," I said.

"It's a sensible question," he said.

"No, it isn't," I said. Quinn knew nothing of marriage

116

or married people. Married people did not ask themselves questions of that kind.

"What did she see when she married you? What did she see before her? She must've thought her life would be happier, otherwise she'd've stayed single or married someone else. She must have thought she would be happier with you than alone. And do you think she has been?"

"Not lately," I said shortly.

"But she's in for the long haul," he said.

"We all are," I said.

He nodded and was silent a moment. I thought that would be the end of it, but I was wrong. "I suppose she saw a man of the world. Literally that, someone who could bring the world to her door. She was not a sophisticated or worldly person. I've always seen her as a woman who's attracted to the fundamentals. I think she wanted someone to bring the world to her door but she wanted *him*, not the world. What she got was the world. And he happened to be part of it, and at times indistinguishable from it. That was part of the trouble, I think it bothered her that she couldn't tell where the world ended and you began. Or vice versa."

"Quinn," I said.

"It must have seemed like such a hell of a good idea. A *beau geste,* and brave. Going back to fundamentals in the woods, I can remember your telling me about it at the time. Sounded dandy and attractive. And I knew it wouldn't work. Everyone did. And the problem wasn't her, it was you. You'd spent so much time looking out that you never learned to look in. You thought what was out there was a hell of a lot more interesting than what was in here." He tapped his chest and smiled. "So you never looked."

I said, "The married life is more complicated than you know."

But he wasn't listening. His hand was in his beard, and his eyes fixed on the middle distance. "But the women look, they look all the time. They look in, we look out. At least that's the way it is with women our age. God knows where Marty looks; maybe she doesn't look anywhere. What she meant by getting back to the fundamentals was getting inside. You and she both. That's what she thought she had to have if life with you was going to be better than life alone, and she thought the way to do that was to retreat from the world. Except you had the war to bring with you, that was part of the bargain. Your obsession puzzled her and then frightened her because it was so remote from her experience. She doesn't know what's in that last chapter, but she supects, and suspicions're always worse than the fact, except in this case; and she knows that, too. What happens next? How much farther away can you get? It's regressive and scatterbrained to retreat, and if there's one thing your wife isn't it's a scatterbrain. So she's scared to death. She and Marty both, though in different ways and for different reasons. However, that's where you are in this and I don't envy your position."

Quinn was much better with other people than he was with himself; many writers of fiction are, and perhaps that is why they are writers of fiction. They are always writing what they don't know about the people they know as if they did know, and making people believe it. And Quinn was not shy about expressing his opinions. I had listened to him carefully, even to the formal "however" at the end. I hated to think of women cornered or frightened. And I did not think of myself as a man of the world, either in the usual sense or in Quinn's sense, though of course there was a nasty kernel of truth in what he said; usually there was, though what he didn't know about me would fill an encyclopedia. But there was no answer I could give him and, truthfully, Quinn didn't want one. As to what my wife saw when she married me, I had no idea. I had no idea of her vision of the future, either. Quinn was correct about that one thing. I had never asked.

I said, "Have you ever been obsessed?"

"All the time," he said. "My books, Plumb. There's a

point, I get deep enough into a book, I'm obsessed by it. The people, what they're doing and how they're doing it and what they want; the awful scrapes they're in. I forget that it's me who put them there. It's more real than my own life and more interesting. And a lot more fun."

"Other than books," I said.

He looked at me. "No."

I tipped my can of beer in his direction, a toast. I said, "Confusion to the enemy," and drank. Of course he had never had an obsession, his life was too full. His rooms were crowded, there was no space for an obsession. An obsession needed emptiness, long vistas, spectacular twilights, and unrealized desires. A certain amount of sexual tension was helpful also, as you approached the giddy precipice. Quinn was the decoy sheep; he left obsessions to his dimmer fellow creatures. I said, "It is not fun, living in service to an obsession. Fun doesn't come into it. But it can be dangerous and lively."

He said, "Self-destructive."

I said, "That, too."

He shook his head, disgusted. He liked to think of me as he thought of himself, a practical man, a professional; now I was letting down the side. He said, "I suppose you think she's going to write the last chapter for you. Or become the Great Muse. It would be like you, to believe something like that. That isn't the way books get written. You're an amateur. Listen a minute to a professional. This is what I do for a living so I'm entitled to talk about it. Your book's your own business, but let me give you a clue. Little Marty's not going to write it for you."

I said, "There's something you don't get. Maybe you'll never get it. There is no difference between that book and my life." I waited for him to react and when he didn't I added, fiercely, *"There is no difference between them at all."*

"She knows that," Quinn said evenly. "That's the trouble. That's what's wrong, and that's what you don't see up there on your precipice. You're so damn dependent on the

119

height. . . ." He paused and threw up his hands, as if uncertain how to continue; but I knew what was coming, and I would listen to it as I would listen to any practical man expatiate. It would be more for his benefit than for mine; he had long since convinced himself that the war in Vietnam was pointless, and he had discarded it as any man of the world would discard a youthful indiscretion. He could not understand those of us who could not let it go—who were, as he said, "Stuck in the tar." We were bad poker players; we clung, hoping to fill an inside straight. Quinn was quite a man with a metaphor.

And of course he observed it from another, older civilization. This was a civilization that did not embrace the future but crouched before it, fearful with the pessimism of the middle-aged. So it was necessary to devalue America's unsuccessful war; that is, integrate it into the world's legacy of unsuccessful wars. "Where is it written that Uhmurrica does not fight lousy wars? Live in Europe awhile, this country looks and feels like a kindergarten, a vast playpen, so careless, self-righteous, and rude, so spoiled, crying over broken toys. So self-absorbed. You were there and I wasn't, so I suppose you think that makes me the priest at the orgy, dispensing technical advice on the positions of the Kamasutra. . . ." I listened to him, winding down at last, thinking that it was a great division, those who attended the war and those who didn't. And the enormity of it became obvious later—as a private soldier might have realized, in 1872, where he had been ten years before: "My God, that was *Antietam.*"

In Europe, the war had been an inconvenience and a distraction, conceivably an embarrassment; in America, it had been a cataclysm, the equivalent of Luther's theses or the Western Front. One saw with one's own eyes; no images, nothing counterfeit. I thought that the only thing worse than going to the war was avoiding it; those who were not there had no claim on those who were.

I said, "You have nothing to say to me on this subject."

He nodded at that, accepting it. "I'll get us a couple more beers," he said, and left the room.

The light outside was fading and I turned on the floor lamp. We had talked the afternoon away. I looked again at the photograph of my wife and me, wondering who the other woman was. I looked at her fingers and tried to imagine the rest of her but she was lost to memory. I wondered if the lunch had stayed with her as it had with me, and whether she had a photograph of the occasion; and whether she had forgotten my name as I had forgotten hers. Ten years ago, the war was rancid. I was in Paris to report on the negotiations; it was my last assignment. The war was still being fought, though in reduced circumstances. So many of the combatants were casualties.

Quinn handed me a beer and said quietly, "It's not worth it."

"It is to me," I said.

"Because you were there?"

"Yes," I said. "Just so." For a moment I imagined the war to be like the woman in the picture. In thirty months I had seen only the fingers, and I couldn't imagine the rest; no one had seen it all. Certainly no American had.

He said, "That puts you one up. I guess it does, except it's a dead end. It's like the north country or falling in love with the wrong woman. Or just falling in love." He paused and ran a riff with his left hand on the glass top of the coffee table. "It's a different culture, you know, hers. They don't mix, the two. There's miles and miles of distance between you and the war's only a few feet of that distance. Don't you see that? She doesn't give a damn for the war, one way or the other; it's all ancient history, and she knows all the moves. I don't know how she learned them but she did. She's different than we were at that age." He looked away, silent a moment. "Tessa and I had a theory in the beginning: you two would be good for each other for a while; you'd be well met and there'd be plenty of laughs. What a hell of a mistake, and we should've known better."

"You'd thought it out?" I was surprised.

"Not far enough," he said. He began to drum again on the glass. "Do you know what *she* wants, this one? What her expectations are? How she sees herself, alone and with you? Does she want a world brought to her door and, if so, which world?"

"Quinn," I said, "you think people are like characters in your books, that you can know them as if you'd created them. I didn't create Marty or my wife, either. I don't know what the hell they want. Freud didn't know and I don't."

He said, "I'll tell you one thing they don't want." I waited patiently for another Delphic pronouncement. He said, "They don't want to be fenced with. They want to be let inside and not just inside a small compartment, either. They want to be admitted to all the rooms. They don't like locked doors."

"We'll see," I said.

"And you're trying to leave everything behind, and you can't. And I feel responsible."

I said, "Don't."

"She's not obsessed," Quinn said. "That's the thing I'd like to tell you, and have you believe. I wish to Christ you'd listen. I know what I'm talking about, and not because I think she's one of my characters, because she isn't. It's one of the obvious points about them, people born in the Eisenhower Era. They don't get obsessed. Now I'll stop."

We drank a third beer and a fourth. We talked about the present administration and its puzzling foreign policy, and then about the high cost of living. I told him how cheap it was, burning wood fuel and maintaining your own garden. In the north country in August there was enough zucchini to feed Poland. Of course it was necessary each spring to clear your garden of rocks, many of them the size of footballs; this had to be done each spring. The rock pile beside the garden seemed to grow, then didn't; the rocks seemed to find their way back into the earth, sinking as if in quicksand. Gardening was not a piece of cake. But Quinn was not interested in north-country agriculture. He was worried about the exchange rate, falling, and about the English bank rate, rising. His house in Chester Square was costing him a fortune. The British economy went from bad to worse, with no one in charge. He had bought gold as one hedge and silver as another, but the Swiss ruined the first and the Hunts the second. It was impossible to know the value of things, today to tomorow; even the art market was in chaos. He had had a piece of a real-estate deal in Hamburg that had looked promising; but it had fallen through at the last minute, no one knew why. For the first time in his life, he didn't know where to put his money. He wasn't even sure of the best kind of money to have, dollars or pounds or Swiss francs or deutsche marks or escudos. He thought he would settle for a cottage in the country—Devon perhaps—where there would always be milk, butter, and cheese. Buy the house outright so there'd be no question of foreclosure— except for an American that was difficult. God knows he would never want to live in *this* white elephant, his Amer- ican office. So there was that to worry about, along with his loans to various friends. Quinn was a soft touch and knew it. Swig Borowy once called him the Federal Reserve. Of course there was always the possibility of selling Chester Square—that is, if there were a buyer for it—and moving to Ireland, where the taxes would be nil. But moving to Ireland meant living with the Irish and there was always the possibility of violence. None of these options —that was the way he thought of his financial life, an options market— was foolproof. In the old days there was always something foolproof.

"Well," he said, smiling gamely, shifting gears. "I hope it works out. I surely do."

"What makes them so different?" I asked.

He made a loud noise, halfway between a grunt and a laugh. "No memory, that's what makes them so different and so attractive, the young. That, and their power of pos- itive thinking and their editor's pencil. They edit out what they don't like or can't understand or interferes with them. There's too much news in their heads, so much instability. They think the world began the day before yesterday and might end the day after tomorrow and that gives them a certain purchase on things that we don't have and'll never have. They don't like history."

"I'm serious," I said.

He gave me a look that said he knew I was and that he was serious, too. I smiled. There wasn't much farther we could take it. Quinn opened two more beers and we sat in silence. Then he began to talk about his house and the things he'd bought since I'd seen it last. He'd collected a number of new pictures.

I said, "I like the Beckmann."

He nodded and said he'd bought the poster in a shop off the Portobello Road, knowing it would be perfect for the guest room. It wouldn't fit in Chester Square, it was definitely a north-country image, the artist austere in black tie, a cigarette with its long ash smoldering in his left hand, the eyes cold and haunted.

I looked at him. "German Artworks of the Twentieth Century."

He smiled. "No doubt."

I said that I had never been to Germany but I planned to visit soon. There was much to see in Germany.

"I've gotten fond of the Krauts lately," he said. "I listen to Wagner all the time, mostly when I'm working. I used to listen to Bix and Bechet and Billie and Willie the Lion. Not any more, and I don't know what it means. Wagner's blues, dum-de-dum-dum. Though when you think about it, *Tannhauser*'s a sort of Kraut *Ain't Misbehavin'*."

eight

It snowed again that night and the next day and the next night. New England had been caught in the usual vice, an Atlantic storm moving north meeting a Canadian storm moving southeast; a head-on collision. According to the radio five people were known dead and three others were missing in coastal towns from Connecticut to Maine. There were no dead in the north country. I could believe it, mountain people knew how to live out a storm. Mountains, massive and immobile, were friendlier than restless seas. When the power failed, there were kerosene lamps at hand and of course the wood stove was not affected; we always kept plenty of wood indoors. But you were on your own in the mountains, and it was nearly always wise to stay put. Mountains were unforgiving of error or insult. Like a cruel Mafia don or silent Buddha, they demanded respect.

I took my coffee to the living room and looked out the window. The sky was gray and there was a wind, but the snow was over. It was not the worst time to be in the north country, during a three-day blow, one low-pressure system after another tumbling down from Canada. There were times when we checked the thermometer as often as you looked at the clock, it being necessary to know exactly how bad it was; that was part of the fun. The news, acquired by por-

125

table radio, was laughable in its irrelevance—a debate at the United Nations, the price of gold, a presidential press conference, the standings in the NFL. We always waited impatiently for the news to end so we could listen to the weather; the forecast was less interesting than the report, what had happened and where. Where had it been coldest and how cold had it been and how much snow had fallen and where and how it compared to the previous year. We depended on statistics. And at the end of the blow, we opened our doors to a pristine world; the firs in my backyard, draped with snow, looked like old women in hoop skirts. It was so beautiful. And then, usually in the late morning, the refrigerator would begin to hum, and we would know that the power had been restored. The furnace would ignite with a pop, and shortly thereafter the phone would ring. Everyone there all right? Anyone there want to go cross-country skiing?

Later in the day, we would hear stories. Somewhere in the valley a house had burned down. The owners lived in Boston. No one had known about the fire until the storm ended. The cause was undetermined but the house was a total loss, being built of wood and Sheetrock in the style of a chalet. Such houses went up "like match factories." Along the main road there were cars in ditches, no casualties, however. The local people were used to it. The tourist season did not begin for another week. Skiers from Boston and New York did not know how to drive in the north country, even when there was good weather. During the Christmas-and spring-vacation holidays the ditches looked like used-car lots in Frankfurt. The second-largest item in our town's budget was for roads, plowing and salting "for the goddamned turkeys." We all laughed at the sight of beautifully gotten-up men and women with their shovels, struggling to free the Mercedes or BMW from the snowbank on the hairpin turn of the access road to the slopes. The roofs of the cars would be festooned with skis and often the children would remain in the car while the parents dug. Everyone had the petulant look of those who feel they are doing work that is beneath them.

The first snow of the season, everyone turned to. It was a great event. All the major roads and lanes would be clear by late afternoon. The state liquor store did a brisk business all day long, selling half-pints of strawberry brandy to the men working the snow-removal equipment. For my son and his friends, a big snow meant three days of vacation from school. For my wife and me, it meant three days of close quarters.

I heard a noise in the kitchen, Marty.

At the end of the blow we made it a family custom to prepare a special dinner, a roast beef with Yorkshire pudding and plenty of spuds, and a good bottle of wine. Often we invited our neighbor, a bachelor whom my wife felt did not eat properly. He would arrive on snowshoes with two quarts of his rancid homemade beer, which we would feel obliged to taste and compliment, before returning to our own drinks.

Upstairs, Tessa called to Quinn.

Marty said shyly, "Hello, there."

I was still in my own house and having difficulty returning to Quinn's. I said, "Have a cup of coffee."

She said, "It's filthy out."

I said, "Not too bad,"

"Raw," she said, and shivered. "What are you doing, standing there?"

"Woolgathering," I said, smiling. I remembered the Thurber cartoon.

She smiled and walked back to the kitchen. Tessa was already there. I heard a chair scrape and low conversation. I turned back to the window. It was early for a winter storm; Christmas was still two weeks away. And of course this would set the tone for the rest of the season, "a bad one." The proprietors of the ski areas would be happy, however. There was the prospect now of good pre-Christmas business, and the holiday would be fine, too, so long as there was no thaw. I put down my coffee cup and went to the telephone and dialed. When my son answered, tears filled my eyes and I could hardly speak. There was a hum in the wire; it was as if I were calling from another continent. In the event, I didn't have to talk for several minutes. Stories tumbled from him, one after the other, about the storm and how they had survived it. The power had been off for eighteen hours, and he and his mother had slept downstairs, in sleeping bags next to the stove. Still, it had been cold, so cold. He had been up since five that morning, awakened by the wind, blowing hard in the last few hours of darkness. And the fire was so low, almost dead, that he had gotten up and stoked it and replenished the woodbox from the run in the garage. It was cold there, too, and he had dropped a stick on his bare foot, a humongous hurt, his toe had turned bright red; and Mom never woke up. It was a heavy stick of maple, dry as tinder; it was the first stick on the fire. Everything was quiet now, but wow! it had been an excellent storm, the worst he'd ever seen, worse even that the one— when was it, Dad?

I said that was the storm of two years ago, or was it three? A spring storm, as I remembered it. The years ran together in the north country, marked only by the quality of the weather and the trips out. That was the year we went to France! It was easy to confuse the seasons, one year to the next. I asked him if they had cut the Christmas tree yet, and he said they were waiting a day or two. There was a little embarrassed silence, and I knew he wanted to ask me why I had gone, where I was, and when I was coming home; but he knew also that he wouldn't like the answers to any of those questions, so he said nothing, holding his breath, hoping that I would volunteer. When I did not reply, he did not press. We were a subtle and considerate family, and we understood that there was terrain in our common life that was better left unexplored.

"Oh," he said at last. "Gosh, Dad. It was something. You should have been here."

I replaced the receiver and returned to the window. I wasn't looking at anything. I heard the voices of the women in the kitchen and Quinn upstairs. Tessa said something and Marty laughed; the house seemed suddenly to brighten, animated by women's voices and the smell of bacon cooking. I watched the town plow make its rounds, the third time in three days. He plowed the road and the driveway up to Quinn's Land-Rover. The rest of it was our responsibility.

I went to the phonograph, chose a record at random, and put it on the turntable. Art Tatum's piano, and I turned the volume low; the room continued to brighten, under the influence of Tatum. Marty appeared at the door, a mug of steaming coffee in her hand. She was wearing ski tights and a T-shirt with a beer company's logo, and the fedora pulled low over one eye. She didn't see me standing in the corner shadows by the phonograph. I watched her hips move to the beat of the music. She stepped to the center of the room to the perimeter of the dusty sunlight, and did a little, slow two-step, snug and concentrated; her feet barely moved at all. I watched her, trying to see beyond her appearance to her essence. What part of her was my own invention? I knew that I had a tendency to use women as vessels, filling them with my own illusions; I wanted them to clear a space inside, room for me; a room away from home. Surely this is a common desire. Without illusions life would be unbearable, a bleak landscape of fact; one's life would be a matter of fact. Of course one cannot always choose one's illusions, many arrive unbidden and linger past their time. I was determined to see inside, to the very center of her, but her singular appearance—those tights, that hat—kept getting in the way, a curtain that obscured her; and obscuring her, it obscured me as well.

She turned suddenly. "You're spying again."

I smiled and shook my head.

"Yes, you were. Admit it. It was just like last night and you know I don't like it. It's—"

"Furtive," I said.

"Sneaky," she said. "Like, a person can't be looking over her shoulder every minute. Does it turn you on?"

That was not an expression I cared for. "No," I said. Not in the way she thought.

She said, "Me, either." She put her coffee mug on the mantel. "You were on the phone a long time."

"My son," I said.

"And how is your son?"

"Great," I said. She smiled skeptically. "Just great." I paused, imagining him in the garage collecting firewood in his bare feet, stumbling and dropping a stick on his toe and yelling in his high, boy's voice, "SHITFUCKPISS-CUNT!" The combination never failed to amuse me, even as I shook my finger at him and told him never to use those words—that word—again and this time I really mean it, Buddy. I said, "He's cheerful. He survived the storm. They both did, he and his mother." Marty nodded, turning, looking at me sideways from under the brim of her hat. Her expression was inscrutable. She was standing against the mantel in an athlete's focused posture, feet a bit apart, arms crossed at her belly. She raised herself on tiptoe, held a moment, then lowered herself. I said, "They had a very big blow down there, worse than here. The power went off, no electricity, no furnace. No toilets, no lights. We missed that."

"Lucky us," she said.

"That's what it means, going back to fundamentals in the north country. A sleeping bag next to the fire and piss-ing in the snow when the power's off." She was on her toes again, balancing. I lit a cigarette, blowing a smoke ring that hung in the still air. "They say it builds character in children."

"Who need it most," she said.

"You learn things here." I blew another smoke ring. I said, "It's not Venice." She looked at me oddly. "And we're plowed out," I said.

"We are? Lucky, lucky us."

"Quinn's dogsbody. He was here just a while ago." I

turned the volume up a notch. It was a Tatum-constructed "Paper Doll," great bunches of chords connected by thrilling runs. I watched her move up and down on her toes, steady and fluid as a machine; she moved as if she were oiled. I had had no success in seeing inside, and now I gave it up. I said, "You're looking . . . very beautiful this morning." She smiled, the curtains parting, then closing.

"I had a nice time last night," she said, then giggled self-consciously. "I'm not having much success in figuring this out."

I said, "We always have a good time together."

"Not always," she said.

I ignored that. "It's worth trying to figure out," I said.

She shook her head, unconvinced. "Why? Explain that. I don't know if it is or not. I think maybe it isn't, if you want to know what I think. Maybe you don't."

"I do," I said.

"The more we talk the heavier it gets and the less I like it. I don't like it much right now." She opened her mouth as if to say something else, then didn't. But she was looking at the telephone on the coffee table.

"It's an illusion," I said.

She leaned forward on one foot. "It is?"

"Sure."

"An illusion that it's heavy?"

"The whole thing's an illusion. That's what it is, it's a kind of dream world." I explained to her about the need for illusions, and how I had been trying to see into her and failing, obstructed by her appearance.

"If you could see inside, what do you think you'd find?"

"A good country," I said. Then I laughed. "A great society."

"Your illusion," she said. She didn't get the reference. I said, "Yes."

She nodded at that. "Okay, fine. But when the illusion goes *poof!*—when that happens, *as it's bound to,* who disappears?"

"We do," I said, improvising. "You and I together. We both disappear."

"I'm not sure I like your illusions," she said.

"Well—" I began.

"The hell with it." She turned away. "What I mean is. I wish you'd just *answer*. What are you doing up here? Really. *Really*, what is it? What is it with me? If it's sex, I can understand that. I mean if it's a *thing*, a weekend thing, a week thing. Something temporary and easy, that's fine. Look, I can deal with that." Her voice softened and she smiled. "It's fun and healthy. Harmless." I smiled back, her choice of words always amused me. She paused, then pointed at the telephone. "Is he a nice boy?"

"Very," I said.

"What's he like?" she asked.

"A good heart," I said. "He has a good heart."

"Is he like you?"

I thought a moment. Then I said, "I don't know."

"I'll bet he is," she said. "You have a good heart."

I said, "So do you."

She said quickly, "I'm sorry I was so . . . difficult, back there. I get like that sometimes. I don't mean to do it. I just want to know where I stand. This place." She looked around the room; dust was floating in the shafts of sunlight, which now had reached the white piano. "It's not what I'm used to. Putting it mildly."

I said, "We can go skiing and talk about it. I'll take you to dinner—"

"Why aren't you home with your boy?"

"Because I'm here," I said. "And he's with his mother."

"And they get along?"

"Very well," I said.

"They're friends?"

"Very good friends," I said.

She rapped sharply on the mantel, twice, with her knuckles.

"They hack around together, ski together, do this and that."

She said, "I really am sorry."

"My fault as much as yours."

"It makes me feel weird."

"It's not your fault," I said.

She looked at me bleakly. "Thanks a bunch."

I tenderly took her arm and we moved away to the window. The sun was brilliant on the snow; it hurt my eyes to look at it. Miraculous Tatum was still in the air and we could hear Quinn and Tessa in the kitchen. I began to talk, beginning at the beginning—or one beginning, an arbitrary beginning. I thought of myself as a painter starting a canvas, painted from the lower left or upper right for no rational reason; the hand that held the brush moved tentatively in that direction and then, gathering confidence, advanced. There was no model for this painting; it was drawn from the mind's eye. I wanted her to understand that she bore no responsibility for our situation, or my situation. It was always a mistake to accept responsibility that was not rightly yours, almost as big a mistake as shifting responsibility that was. Really, I wanted to absolve her of any guilt, so the picture I painted was a pretty pastoral, as pristine as the snowdrifts outside Quinn's house. She listened quietly and did not interrupt. I described her again as I had seen her the first night, how she looked to me; this was an artist's license. I explained that I was trying to work myself back to a time in the war when my own life had made sense to me, what I did with it and what I expected from it. It was not war itself because I was not a war lover, far from it; so it was something else, something I had lost and now must find. She was the key to it; her key, my lock. Perhaps it was her discord, a discord of trumpets, her randomness, her potential, and the danger she represented. I wanted to believe that we were all of good heart, though infatuated.

I looked at her, and recollected again that moment of

133

vast stillness before the explosion when every sense was stretched tight, electrified. Of course this was in the mind only, an illusion, and more real for being an illusion. I took her hand and told her that I thought I could find my younger self in her, and not a younger sexual self but a younger moral self. With her I was me without my memory—without injury and without compromise, and unafraid. The difficult we do today, the impossible takes a little longer. Stay alert, stay alive. I explained about my last chapter, unconceived, unwritten. The last chapter would guarantee the first. The book was autobiography but I would appear nowhere in it. It was a history of the war, pure and simple.

I believed what I was saying and was persuasive because after a few moments she began to relax. Her hand was soft in mine. She put her arm around my back and squeezed, a friend's gesture of support. We stood together in the country silence, looking into Quinn's snowy driveway, the snow crystals sparkling in the sun. She raised herself on tiptoe, put her head on my shoulder, and sighed.

"You can't know what it was like," I said, conscious that this was an ambiguous statement, surreal in its way, like one of Picasso's hole-in-the-head women.

"No," she said, "I surely can't. But I have a feeling I'm going to."

We kissed. I began to talk excitedly about the runs at Stowe—Goat, Star, National, the difficult runs, expert trails. I spoke of them familiarly, having heard about their characteristics for years. I said I wanted to watch her ski the Goat, a murderous two-thousand-foot vertical fall. We could be at Stowe in two hours, if we hustled. We'd take her car; the day was perfect, the clouds all had disappeared now.

"All right, all right," she said.

I said, "Let's go."

She turned to face me. "I don't know how much of it I believe," she said. I held my breath. "I don't know how much of it *you* believe. Enough, I guess." She laughed shortly and shook her head, moving to the center of the room and then to the corner where the phonograph was. She stood in the shadows, watching me. Then she began to whisper, so softly I could not hear the words. She was talking to herself in a seductive undertone. In a second she was across the room and facing me. She suddenly threw her arms around my neck and kissed me. Nothing moved in the room. She held my face in her hands and whispered, "This is so much fun. You're so much fun. I like you so much. Why can't this go on forever?"

nine

In the event we decided against Goat, Star, or National.
I had not been on skis in years and those trails were haz-
ardous to life, though Marty skied them every day. We as-
cended instead to Nosedive, it being an invariable of eastern
ski areas that the more ominous and forbidding the name,
the easier the trail, and of course the reverse was also true.
There were not many people, surprising for so fine a day.
Nosedive was situated almost at the summit and com-
manded a wide view of the trails. I looked down, left and
right, at the chair lifts lacing the mountain together. I
watched them intently, slowly moving miniature chairs
suspended above the slopes; they looked so flimsy in their
bright colors, and surreal against the white of the snow.

Marty was whistling happily and fussing with her boot.
I continued to stare at the chairs, my memory nagging at
me, trying to remember what it was about them that was
so familiar. Then I remembered and laughed out loud. Two
years before, my wife and I had taken a winter trip to Europe
and spent a weekend in Paris. She had taken up jogging
that year and insisted on running in the Tuileries each
morning. She ran counterclockwise, commencing down the
Seine-side of the garden to the Louvre, then back below the
rue de Rivoli. I remained at the fountain near the Jeu de

Paume, smoking a cigarette, shivering, bored, watching her run. It was very cold and the water in the fountain was frozen. Beneath the surface of the ice were dozens of the garden's yellow wrought-iron chairs with their cello-shaped backs. I supposed they had been thrown there by vandals, but in my imagination I saw them as part of a stage set, props ordered by Buñuel or Fellini for a preposterous movie; they gave a ludicrous, surreal look to the fountain. One looked at them and expected to see a frozen actor as well. Now, looking at the chairs suspended on cables high above the slopes at Stowe, I was reminded of the fountain in the Tuileries, the cold, the city smell, and the green rooftops of the rue de Rivoli.

I laughed again and Marty looked at me and smiled. "It's great, isn't it?"

"Sure is," I said. I was cold and scared and hoped I could find my way down on an easy trail. I decided to tell her about the yellow chairs in the fountain at the Tuileries, but either I told the story badly or she missed the connection because she neither laughed nor commented. While I told the story, she limbered up, concentrating on getting loose. Her inattention irritated me, and I thought of going on with the story, inventing if necessary. Perhaps a conversation with Jean Gabin or Jeanne Moreau, a miraculous sexual encounter, champagne in the bar of the Crillon later . . .

She said, "You look good." She nodded approvingly. "You look good in ski gear, very trim. This was a great idea and we'll see how you do, and if you're in form we'll try some of the tougher trails later on. This is really easy, it's a bubble-gum trail."

"Okay," I said.

She said, "You go first."

I wanted a cigarette so badly, but they were tucked away in an inside pocket and it would take five minutes to get to them. "No, you," I said. "I want to watch, see how you do it. I'll meet you at the bottom, or halfway down, or whatever."

"Just take it slow," she said.

"See you at the bottom," I said.

"Not *too* slow," she said.

"Right," I said. I smiled encouragingly and turned to say something more, but she was looking over my shoulder and smiling. A crowd of young skiers was approaching, very colorful in bright parkas and cowboy hats. A boy in a red parka had a portable radio slung around his neck, the volume high; country music, *twang twang*. However, the music was not as loud as their laughter. They were passing a joint. One of them waved at Marty and called her name and she waved back. She made a motion for them to go ahead, but they wanted conversation first. One of them was having trouble with his bindings, so there was general talk about bindings. Geze bindings, Salomon bindings, Markers, Burts, and other bindings whose manufacturers I did not recognize. One of the men had new skis and there was a general discussion of those, Atomics, Heads, Olins, Fischers, Authiers.

At last they prepared to go, scissoring away down the slope with shouts and promises to meet at the base for a drink. The boy in the red parka gave a thumb's-up sign and called to Marty, "Bye-bye, beautiful!" She laughed and raised her hand in a clenched-fist salute. They were good skiers, plunging straight down, then swooping in wide arcs. It took a minute for the country music to fade and for the silence to settle again. I was cold and somehow weary. We said nothing, waiting for her friends to disappear. Marty wore a funny little smile, one that reminded me of a parent watching a child take his first steps; she was following her friends down the mountain with her eyes.

"Ready?" she said.

"Absolutely," I said.

Then she was away, gone so quickly I scarcely realized it, disappearing over a lip. I retained an image of her, hair flying, body bent low in a tuck, snow spraying. She was gorgeous to watch, leaning this way and then that, her body almost parallel to the ground. She was dressed in blue—navy blue boots, pants, parka, sweater under the parka, and a white silk scarf around her neck. The beauty and the beast, I was so shabby in my corduroys and black sweater and rented equipment. Her ensemble was completed by coal-black goggles fastened around her head by a white elastic band. She wore no ski cap and the white band was nearly invisible in the thicket of her hair. She had disappeared and then I saw her again, out from under the lip below me, flying, in complete control, running dead straight as if she were on rails. She did not look back.

It was a long way down, almost half a mile. At least we were not on Goat. I did not like the thought of being out of control on this slope. It was all a matter of caution and technique, controlling the environment; but I did not have the technique, I had never had it. I shuffled forward and was away, immediately picking up speed. Astonishing, I thought, how you picked up velocity so quickly. I tried to remember what you were supposed to do. I knew you were supposed to "feel your edge." If you felt your edge, you were in control; edges were supposed to be like cat claws and you clung to the mountain with them. I was dragging my poles, trying to slow down. Then it didn't seem to matter and I went into a crouch, turned, and stopped. It was perfectly done, to my astonishment, and I was standing in the silence watching the other skiers. I was no longer cold; and I had not fallen or made a fool of myself. In fact I had come to a rather elegant stop, and no matter that this stop had accurred only ten or fifteen seconds after I had begun my run. I had proved that I could stop, and this was not inconsequential; it was my trouble, stopping.

My goggles fit awkwardly over my eyeglasses. I adjusted them and began again, slowly, a long traverse of the slope and back. It was a lazy man's descent and with each turn I grew more confident, feeling my edge. I even dared look around, it was spectacularly pretty this high; the sun was resting on the summit of the mountain. Someone had once told me that you should ski as if carrying a bag of groceries under each arm, and in that way your elbows would never lock. I remembered that advice, moving faster now, often lifting my downhill ski for balance. I shot over a low mogul and instantly found myself in trees, rushing down a trail that should not have been there. I had been looking the other way and had not seen the trees, and I was unused to goggles, with their limited vision; and of course, and first, I was besotted with success. She'd said, "You look good in ski gear, very trim. . . ." A gent in corduroy trousers and a black sweater, no Bogners for this pro—an advert for Ski Vermont, me and perhaps Suzy Chaffee executing tandem christies. The trees had come from nowhere, and the narrow trail through them seemed to lead nowhere except down. I was no longer feeling my edge or much of anything except terror; I did not like speed. Speed kills. I ducked my head to avoid a branch, at the same time trying to find the center of the trail, altogether safer. I wanted to lock myself into the tracks but my knees would not obey. My legs commenced to tremble and I felt my coordination coming apart as if I were a marionette whose master had dropped the strings. I avoided a rock oucropping to my right and crouched even lower, wanting the lowest possible center of gravity on the theory that when I fell, as I knew now that I would, I could keep my extremities close to my body and my body close to the earth. Probably it was instinctive, a fetal position for the fall. I tried to move forward on my skis in order to regain some control, but I was pulled backward, recoiling as one would recoil from a fist. My skis were fat on the snow and without life. The trees were all around me, dense firs and leafless birches, so thick it seemed there could be no trail at all. Then I flew out of the trees, a branch scraping my head, and was abruptly on the downhill slope, moving faster than I have ever moved on skis. I was sweating like a pig and breathing hard, completely out of control; I was passive and the slope was active, and there

140

seemed nothing for me to do but give myself to it. Below me I could see the gate house and the short lines of skiers waiting for the lift. None of them was looking at me, but I raised one hand—I thought of the imaginary groceries spilling, littering the trail—to warn them all, though of what I could not say. I was still well up the hill, and in that moment I realized I was still on my feet, skiing. My eyeglasses were skewed inside the goggles and I could not see properly. But I knew I had not fallen. Precarious as my balance was, I was not down-and-out. I tried to center what strength I had left. I thought that if I could focus my energy, bring it all in service to a turn to the left and a full stop— then I would be safe and unharmed and this nightmare would end. If I could make the turn as I had made it before, repeat the motion exactly, I would defeat the mountain. The mountain was trying to destroy me. I had a taste of copper pennies in my mouth and my vision was blurred, but my mind was racing—calculating the angles and the right place to bring it all to a halt, whoosh in a shower of snow, a manly reassertion of control, a triumph of the will, no less. . . .

I was falling and then down, tumbling. One ski released and flopped around my ankle. The mountain rose up at me, my right shoulder hit first, and then I was on my back. I had no wind. Snow was everywhere, inside my goggles and my trousers and collar. I lost a mitten, and then the goggles spun away, my glasses inside them. I was blind without my glasses, my vision collapsed into fragments of light, everything blurred around the edges. I slid for a hundred miles and half my lifetime, on my back headfirst, over one mogul and then another, finally coming to rest as slowly and smoothly as a train entering a station.

"Jesus Christ," somebody said.

"Don't move him." I recognized the voice.

"Jesus H. Christ."

"Wait'll the ski patrol—"

"I'm all right," I said.

"No you're not." I squinted to see who it was, the man with the familiar voice. It was the boy in the red parka, the radio around his neck; country music, *twang twang*.

"I'm fine," I said. I put my hand to my face and it came away sticky and warm. I moved one leg and then the other. No damage as far as I could tell. My left arm was stiff but the other moved all right. I had so many aches and pains I could not sort them out, my legs and back and head, bruises everywhere. I sat up and watched the blood drip into the snow.

"Don't move, for crissakes," the boy in the red parka said. "Ski patrol'll be here in a minute, paramedics. They're good, best in the east. We'll get you out of here on a toboggan."

"Where am I cut?"

"Forehead, left side," he said. "A biggie." He grinned at me. He had even white teeth and a strong jaw, clear eyes and dirty-blond hair like Robert Redford's.

I picked up a fistful of snow and applied it to my forehead, stinging. My head hurt like hell. On the edges of my fuzzy vision I saw an older man pull up and stop. I knew he was a man my age by the way he moved. He squatted on his skis and looked me in the face, up close. I was sitting with my elbows resting on my knees. He asked me if anything was broken and I said no. He didn't ask me if I was sure, only nodded. He lifted my eyelids with his thumb, first one and then the other; blood and melting snow dribbled down my cheeks. He was a gray-haired man with a battered face and pale gray eyes, and a network of lines around the eyes. He smelled of tobacco. I don't know what he was looking for in my eyes, but whatever it was he didn't find it because he grunted once, an affirmation. He fumbled inside his parka and came out with a silver flask and handed it to me.

"That's dumb," the boy in the parka said.

It was a beautiful flask, delicately chased on one side, engraved in block letters on the other. The lettering said

D.D. to C.C. I tipped it in his direction, thanks, and drank. At first the taste was unfamiliar and then I recognized it, a malt whiskey, The Glenlivet, Glenmorangie, Bowmore, one of those.

He said, "Take another."

I thanked him and asked if he had a cigarette. He smiled and gave me a Camel and lit it for me.

"Here they are," the boy said. "The paramedics, thank God."

I looked at my new friend. "Are they any good?"

He said, "They're all right."

He handed me the flask again and I noticed a large ring on the third finger of his right hand. It was the West Point ring.

I said, "As good as the 3rd Field Hospital at Nha Trang?"

He looked at me and grunted. Negative. Then he took back his flask.

The whiskey made a mellow place in my stomach, and I was able to ignore the ache in my head and the other aches. It was good to have a soldier around, a drinking soldier, a soldier who knew something about casualties. I turned to the boy and said, "Where's Marty?"

"Marty," he said. He looked at one of his friends and asked where Marty was. The friend said something I didn't hear. He turned back to me. "She's skiing Goat," he said. "We can send someone off to get her—"

"No," I said. I turned to the soldier, intending to ask him to come down to the lodge for a drink. Perhaps more than one drink, with a face like that he'd know the drill. But he had taken his flask and gone. With my collapsed eyesight I couldn't see him anywhere in the vicinity. Then the paramedics were bending over me with their patient questions. I answered all of them in the negative and they gave me a plaster for my forehead and a form to sign later, and helped me down the trail. I looked every which way for the man with the flask. No doubt we had mutual friends and similar experiences. But he was nowhere to be seen, or

143

at least I didn't see him. So I went to the lodge, figuring I'd find him there. But I saw no one I knew, so I sat quietly at the bar, nursing my aches and pains, waiting for Marty.

◇

That night, after a light dinner, we returned to the big drafty bedroom in Quinn's house. She sat across the room at the vanity table, nude, brushing her hair. I watched her from the bed. She was brushing vigorously to keep away the cold, her back muscles moving rhythmically. This had never failed to arouse me but that night I was distracted. I hurt all over.

Usually she went quietly to sleep, falling unconscious almost immediately after we made love. I always wanted to talk but had to be content with looking at her, in repose in the big bed, stretched out on her back like one's image of an Egyptian pharaoh, expressionless, hands at her sides. But that night she wanted to talk. I tried to concentrate as she explained her study of the exact sciences. She started talking as she climbed into bed, clutching a bottle of mineral water and two glasses. "I have discipline but I want to use it for something else. I don't think I could make a life of physics. Maybe I cared too much about it. And life is not theoretical, is it?" She'd looked coldly at her abilities and decided she was not world-class, and it was important to her to be world-class at anything she did.

Listening to her, I smiled. She sounded like an athlete who'd decided not to turn pro. She had the desire but not the physique. She'd examined her physique and decided she was too short or too slow or not agile enough, owing to unfortunate musculature. It was not something that desire or a rigorous training schedule or superb nutrition could overcome.

"I was very good with theory and with the computer. But . . ." She shrugged, staring at the ceiling, her hands locked behind her head. "It had nothing to do with my life or with any life. I suppose it's the way you're made and what you've come from and what you've experienced and want to experience, expectations-wise, and I liked it all right, theory, but I didn't love it and, like, in the end I didn't respect it much either, theory. I cared a lot, though." She smiled, her eyes on the ceiling. "So for a while I did history. I thought I had the temperament for it because history's *reliable,* you can depend on it."

I said, "No it isn't."

"Of course it is," she said. "History's prophetic, you can use it to foretell the future. It's like watching a random quark, if you could watch quarks. A quark out of control, and if you plot it long enough you can predict its behavior— or that's the theory—no one's actually done it, though there's no good reason why it can't be done. You can plot history because you know where it's been. All that needs doing is to factor in the variables. Then you'll know where it's going. All you have to do is get the variables straight, which no one ever will, probably, in my lifetime. So for now it's not an exact science, that's the zippy thing about it. It's more like an art or a craft. I'm pretty satisfied with it, though America seems so exhausted to me now, all those old *men.* With their loopy memories." She looked at me sideways. "That's why I love the mountain."

I was only half listening. The cut in my forehead stung and my thighs felt as if they were on fire; my wrist was sprained and I'd torn the nail off my little toe. My mouth was swollen, and I could feel a coughing fit coming on. I had agreed that I would never smoke in the bedroom, she hated it so; she hated the smell. I wanted a cigarette so badly. I had one pack in my suitcase and another in the carrybag, and I was trying to figure out how to get to them and sneak one in the bathroom. One cigarette would get me through the night, I was confident of that.

"And the people who work on it, the instructors and the ski bums. They're very passionate people. They're people with nothing to lose." She laughed. "They're not ready for prime time." When I said nothing, she continued, "And that

145

gives them an edge. They're attractive people to be around, slightly dangerous and a bit off the wall. I'm attracted to them. They don't give one damn." She grinned at me.

"I'd be more sympathetic to them, probably, some other time."

"Well," she said. "They aren't exhausted." I knew that this was a declaration of some kind and leaned painfully toward her to listen more carefully. My teeth were furry and my lungs tight, though I had forgotten about the cigarette. "There's something about us all being together on the mountain, it's so neat. I love the cold weather and being first off the mountain early in the morning, the sun just beginning to rise, virgin powder, no tracks. We call it dancing, when we're skiing together, and that's just what it is, we're doing a ballet to each other's shadows. It's like making love. Making love to the mountain, and there's nothing to think about except how you're moving, moving light, so's you can hardly feel the terrain underneath, it's the marriage of heaven and earth and the mountain's your lover. I'm—" She sighed. "—so bloody tired of school and study. *Studying* to be this, *studying* to be that. I want to *do*. She does, therefore she is." Marty looked at me hard, touching my mouth with her fingers. "Very different," she said.

"What?" I had missed the reference.

"Us. I'm not sure we believe the same things."

"If you mean the mountain, we don't."

"I didn't," she said. "But we can add that to the list."

That fucking mountain. But wasn't she full of surprises? In other circumstances I would have been interested, in the same way I would want to hear from a scientologist or a Republican. But my forehead hurt and I couldn't arrange my right hand in such a way as to neutralize the sprain, so I held my wrist awkwardly. I thought to myself that it would be easier if she had been a provo, involved with PFLP or Fatah or Black September—any of those. Perhaps the IRA, though that would be less likely. She was too shirty and would never take orders. If she had been a provo instead of a skier we could talk about weapons—Brens, Stens, Thompsons, Kalashnikovs, Brownings. I thought of her suddenly in a kaffiyeh, an AK-47 over her shoulder, sunburned and trim. She would be part of a reconnaissance team, her long-distance running a valuable asset; she could go *Nordique* if they ever decided to kidnap the King of Norway. With her dark hair and black eyes she would fit right in, only her loping American walk a giveaway. Instead, she was an athlete, making love to a mountain. Well, the mountain had fucked me; no reason she couldn't fuck it.

"Why are you smiling?"

I said, "My head hurts." I touched the bandage, thinking of it suddenly as a badge of honor. Once in the Zone I had seen a captured Viet Cong, a young woman. Her right shoulder was heavily bruised from the kick of the weapon; that was how they knew she was a guerrilla. When they ripped her shirt off and saw it, she smiled. She might as well have been wearing the Order of Lenin. They gave her the shirt back but she refused to put it on. Everyone was looking at her bare breasts, light against the purple of the bruise. She was guarded by two young GIs who were trying to get her away into the woods, until I took an NCO aside and told him and he put a stop to it. She was much tougher and more dangerous than the GIs. ARVN Intelligence took the young woman away in a helicopter, and as she climbed aboard she turned to give me a last look, a snarl with bared teeth. I had taken several pictures of her but missed that one.

She said, "Sometimes the mountain can be unforgiving."

I nodded. That was true enough.

"What do you think about it, as a career?"

"Skiing?" I shrugged, my mind was elsewhere, on my aching wrist and the bandage on my forehead and on the young Vietnamese with the bruised shoulder. I remembered that one of the GIs had an erection and kept calling her attention to it. God knows what she would've done with him. No question they were going to throw her out of the helicopter, and no question that she knew it. And she didn't give a damn, what was one more life given in the cause of the revolution? I said, "As long as it doesn't go on too long, why not?"

"What's 'too long'?"

For that young woman, it had been her lifetime. I said, "I don't know. A couple of years. Trouble with it is, it doesn't lead to anything. You want a career to lead to something. But if you really like it and it satisfies you and you're good at it, why not? Better a first-rate skier than a second-rate historian."

"But I was good at history."

"Well, then," I said. "There you are." Remembering the episode now, there was something provocative about it, the young woman bare to the waist, defiant, surrounded by armed men in battle dress. But at the time there was nothing provocative, only something dangerous; and she was not sexy at all but tough—humorless, hard-muscled, and sly. Sex didn't come into it.

She said, "I hate the rat race. And up here there isn't any of that, there's just the snow and the training for the trials. It's sport, and it's serious. And the people are great, especially the men."

I finally got it. She meant the instructors, bedroom athletes, men in conspicuous good health; some of them were as old as I was, but their balance was superb. I always wondered what they did in the summers. Probably they went to Colorado. I said, "All those Austrians, the north country's Hitler Youth."

"That's a dumb remark."

"You didn't hear them singing the *Horst Wessel* that night in the lodge."

"They were not singing the *Horst Wessel*."

"They were one night, about five years ago. I heard them." This was a lie, or anyway not a verified fact. They were singing in German, though it might have been the pilgrims' chorus from *Tannhauser*. It was grotesque, whatever it was. I began to laugh, which turned into a spasm of coughing. I looked at her, she was sitting still as a statue, the bedsheet up around her neck; her looks enchanted me, there was something of the virgin goddess about her. I took her hand but she pulled it away. I said, "I think it's fine, you on the mountain. The instructors are fine, too. I was joking." I paused, wondering how far to take it. I said, "I think you're so bright and interesting. You look at things so differently. It only occurred to me that it was a waste, you here. I think of you doing something else, I don't know what."

"I told you before, I'm unreliable."

"And I told you before. I wouldn't try to change that. No loyalty oaths, please."

She said, "But you will. They always do." Then she turned away, her face to the wall, and went to sleep.

Later, I stumbled out of bed and had a cigarette in the bathroom. Sitting on the john in the darkness, smoking, I thought of my unhappy school days when I habitually had a cigarette in the stall each evening before lights-out. Smoking was a serious offense, and once I was almost caught; *was* caught, but the house master chose to ignore it. The punishment then was expulsion. Now of course the children smoked dope and had sex together without apparent consequence, or anyway official consequence. The son of one friend had been found with a case of gin in his room and the daughter of another had been found in bed with her boyfriend; both had been let off with warnings and both found the warnings compromising to their civil rights and what the girl called her "personhood." Their parents had been given quite a lecture, however. I began to smile, a familiar thin, rueful, self-conscious smile. It was the smile of one who had been trumped.

There would be consequences for this escapade, a hell of a large bill, time and charges scrupulously accounted for. There would be charges for everyone at my table, even those who had eaten little or who had come and gone without eating at all. The bill would come as a particular surprise to anyone who thought it was my treat. The management insisted that everyone pay, regardless of size, sex, or appetite. I didn't want to think about it, but I knew that I would be paying on the installment plan; more than likely, so would the others. This was the beginning of a ruined economy and a certain amount of moral confusion as well, not to mention the inflation. I was still governed by the old rules, like it or not; and I didn't, much. If I really worked at it, I could break the bank.

And what was I doing now, reprising my school days? The house master was asleep in the next room and I was sneaking a cigarette as though I were a sophomore. Well, I thought it was a beau geste, my run on the slopes. I touched my forehead with my good hand, the one that held the cigarette. Thank God for the old soldier and his flask. God, he was beat up though, and had a world-class vanishing act. I wondered if he had a weakness for the beau geste. From the look of that face, I guessed that he did. With about the same results as mine.

She stirred and called my name. I saw the light under the door and heard the rustle of bedclothes. She would get a bill, too, but it would be in a modern coin. She called my name loudly and I answered, Midnight call of nature, heh-heh-heh.

I stood up, dizzy, hurting everywhere. Guiltily, I threw the cigarette into the toilet bowl and opened the window to dispel the evidence. Standing at the open window looking at the brilliant night sky of the north country, I lit another cigarette, inhaling deeply. I felt no chill, though the night was cold. My thoughts, moving at the speed of light, warmed me. I was irrevocably in her orbit, like any errant star that had slipped its own course, spun out of control and found itself attracted to a powerful sun. So I circled defiantly, torrid at one axis and glacial at the other. Thinking about that, I threw my cigarette into Quinn's driveway, admiring the bold arc and little splash of sparks when it hit the hood of my car and bounced into the snow. Then I limped back into the bedroom, to the arms of my unreliable lover, who was snoring softly.

◇

On Monday night I picked her up at the mountain after work. I had checked us into a motel so we would not have to make the drive north after dinner. My forehead no longer hurt and a weak wrist was my only souvenir of Saturday's run on Nosedive. I wanted us to have a fine dinner and a long talk. I wanted a fat steak and a spud and a bottle of wine, perhaps two, so we went to an old favorite of mine, a restaurant with leather banquettes and a fireplace and a sign out front that said

STEAKS CHOPS SEAFOOD COCKTAILS.

It had the best salad bar in the north country and a serious wine list. I announced that I wanted a large meal, a shrimp cocktail and a wedge of pâté before the steak and the cheese board afterward. I thought it would be festive to commence with martinis. She listened to all this without comment, except to say that she would have a glass of white wine instead of a martini. And she would make her own salad, she didn't want red meat or a potato. She complained that the potatoes were always as big as shoes. She had eaten too much rich food, her stomach was upset; she was gaining weight and in the mornings felt blah. It was an offense against her system, so much food. She was a skier; she was supposed to be in training.

I like to stay in shape, she said. She dropped her hands in her lap and looked away. I drank one martini, and we ordered and sat in silence a moment. Wine arrived and she drank listlessly. Presently she smiled, apparently improved; I told her Quinn stories.

Later, I said, "Tell me about Shelby."

"Boring," she said.

"Come on," I said.

"Boring Boring Boring." My shrimp arrived and I dug in. "It's boring."

I pressed. "Tell me about his politics."

She tried without success to suppress a smile. "Don't ask."

"One illustration." I wanted to know more about the men in her life—what they believed in, and the attraction they held for her.

She began to laugh. "He was the inventor of the chain letter."

"Yes," I said. We had finished one bottle of wine and I ordered another.

She said, "The one that would bring down the government. When we were freshmen at Wisconsin. He had this brilliant idea for a chain letter, very intricate and mathematically sound. The thing would begin in Madison and spread through the Big Ten, then jump to the Coast. That was the idea, anyway. Instead of sending money, you'd send savings bonds. U.S. savings bonds, get it?"

I looked at her, baffled. "As a patriotic gesture? At the end of the war?"

"In a manner of speaking, yes," she said. "Idea was, you'd buy the bonds at a discount, right? Government uses the money to finance its disgusting war machine, right? Well, if at a magic moment everyone cashes the bonds— well then, the government's left with commitments it cannot possibly fulfill. It's borrowed on the bonds, get it?" She leaned across the table, toying with her wine glass, grinning. "The idea was to bankrupt the government and it would've worked, too, through the underground, and we thought we had a Rockefeller interested. Except a couple of months after Shelby thought of the idea the bastards ended the draft and that took the juice out of it. No one cared after that. A nifty idea, though. Don't you think?"

I nodded reflexively, thinking of them together in a

dormitory room in Madison, scheming, their merciless hands around the throat of poor old Uncle Sam. She chattered on, something about ruining the capital markets and plunging the country into chaos. I was watching a couple on the other side of the room. They had been looking at us. The woman was slender and beautifully dressed. I guessed they were tourists up from Boston, though there was something familiar about the woman. A little silence had come between them now, not at all strained or unpleasant; it was as if they knew each other so well they had no need to speak and could communicate by thought transference. I wondered if they were lovers or man and wife and decided they were married; of course they were married. Lovers were never silent. These two obviously enjoyed each other's company. They both had beautiful manners, though perhaps that was only because they were so natural with each other. What appeared to be good manners was actually simple affection or fearlessness. And they were married all right, the woman was a friend of my wife. They played tennis together.

Marty was winding down now. Wasn't it a great scheme? She laughed.

"Ha ha," I said. "Coals to Newcastle."

"What do you mean?" She looked at me queerly.

"I mean the country was already on its knees."

"Was it? It didn't seem so if you were eighteen and fucked over by a draft board." I nodded; she had a point. She turned away a moment, then giggled. "Old Shelby, he wanted to rewire history. So did I, then. And maybe I still do. I'll say one thing for him. God, he was good-looking and the sexiest man I ever knew. At Madison he had all the ladies after him, but I won. My dad didn't like him, though. You wouldn't believe the grief from my dad when Shelby and I were shacked up together."

"Yes, I would," I said.

She looked at me without smiling. "Yes, you'd agree about that. You'd agree about everything, that's the trouble. That's our trouble. It'd end up being you and him against me. I feel that anyway, that you're not on my side. I don't feel any support coming from you any more than I feel support coming from him. I feel you're sitting in judgement, waiting for me to make the wrong move or say the wrong thing, so you can correct me. Set me straight. So you'd get along fine, you two. You're just as pessimistic and reactionary as he is."

"Perhaps we had the same kind of war, me and your father."

"Maybe," she said evenly. "My dad's quite a marksman, always takes off the first day of deer season. Always gets his buck with one shot. 'Round,' he calls it. Never goes into details because my mom doesn't like it. And I don't like it, either."

"Sounds like we'd get along."

"Famously." She glared at me over her wine glass. "He's got about a million friends, like you. Everybody loves my dad. He and half a dozen of the million load up the rifles and head for the woods, every opening day. Where we live, it's a slaughter."

"Sounds okay so far."

"It's like you and the horde of journalists heading for the wars, aren't you always there on opening day?"

"Not always," I said.

"They always bring plenty to drink, though they never touch anything until after the day's shoot. The rules about that are very strict, but I doubt it makes much difference to the deer. Just keeps them from shooting each other." She filled her glass and set the bottle down with a bump. "He was damn good about Canada, though, I'll give him that. You're smoking a lot for someone who says he wants to give it up."

"I decided I didn't want to." The couple from the other side of the room were up now and threading their way through the tables to the door. They took a roundabout route so they would not have to pass near our table. The woman gave one quick look around before they disappeared

154

out the door. I watched them go, then turned back to Marty. I felt heavy-bellied, uncomfortable in my clothes. I wondered whether she'd wait for the weekly tennis match or call in the morning.

"It's a filthy habit."

I nodded in agreement.

"Self-destructive," she said.

I nodded again.

"Deer, Communists. What's the difference?"

"The Communists are armed."

She said, "You're damned right they are."

"And the last time out, they won. So that's the second difference."

"Check," she said.

"The person I was giving them up for turned into someone else."

"She's the same person. And that's stupid, it isn't the sort of thing you do for someone else. It's not the act of a Christian martyr, or one of your soldier boys who throw themselves on a hand grenade. It's something you do for yourself. It's your own choice."

I said nothing to that. We sat in a little zone of annoyance, avoiding each other's eyes. All I had wanted to do was have a pleasant dinner, perhaps make her laugh. If we were on the same side, then we could see the other side. I wanted her to know that we were not enemies, and that I was not a terrorist who wished to brutalize or silence her. But we were a bad fit, and with me she could not be her best self.

The waiter had collected our plates and was now at my elbow. He put an austere green salad in front of Marty and gave the steak to me. The baked potato, swaddled in shiny tinfoil, occupied a separate plate. I cut the potato, releasing its steam, and put two pats of butter inside. The waiter ladled sour cream on top of the butter. I asked if there were chives and he said there were none, nor any bacon bits. The sour cream ran over the tinfoil, puddling. Irritated, I turned to the steak. It was a twenty-four-ounce porterhouse, charred

155

on the outside but pink as a rose within. I took a bite and announced that the steak was first class, compliments to the chef.

Marty looked at my plate and said, "That is disgusting."

The waiter said, "*Bon appétit.*"

I couldn't let that pass, and I asked him if he was French. Oh yes, he said. He was a Quebequois. He often translated for his traveling countrymen. I said it was always wise to have a French-speaking person on the premises of a restaurant, it gave everyone confidence. I asked if he had heard the story of the maître d' of the old Pump Room in Chicago, a Frenchman from Lyons who knew the midwestern palate like the back of his own hand. For many years he had been an invaluable employee. He was the one who invented steak *flambé*, or anyway introduced it to the menu of the Pump Room. Asked why he cooked a steak *flambé*, he explained, "The customers like it and it don't hurt the meat none."

When the waiter stopped laughing he said, "Son of a bitch."

"Come on," I said. "Where are you really from?"

"Winooski," he said, "Working my way through U-V-M."

"Let me guess," I said. "French literature."

"Political science," he said.

Marty said, "I would like some oil and vinegar for my salad." She had sat watching us, listening but not smiling. With a flourish, the waiter produced cruets. Then, with a smile and a nod at me, he moved off. I watched Marty pour the oil and vinegar, then sit back, her hands in her lap. I began to eat my steak, but the fun had gone out of it. The waiter was a nice kid, though. I tried to remember where I had heard the story of the steak *flambé* and couldn't. I remembered the last time I told the story, though; it was at the Erawan in Bangkok and the girl I was with had laughed and laughed.

Marty poured a glass of wine and sat staring at her plate. She lifted her head slowly, as if pressed by a great weight. She moved her shoulders and took a deep breath. I think the weight was me; I think she thought I would devour her. I think she saw the shadow of me over her, a shadow that came on forever, and she had no power to divert it or do anything with it except watch it—so long and dark, so heavy, dangerous, and menacing.

I thought she would make some comment on my conversation with the waiter, but when she spoke it was to resume our conversation where it left off. "You do things for yourself, not for the approval of others. Like this, you'll find it trivial and adolescent. It doesn't measure up to your search-and-destroy missions. When Shelby and I were on the barricades. In a manner of speaking. It doesn't seem very important now, our little boutique revolution; but it had a meaning then. It had a meaning for him and for me and for us together, and we were very together at that time, believing that our government was the most dangerous government in all the world, all those nice well-heeled Americans, people like you and Quinn, indifferent, arrogant . . . Where was I? Yes, the FBI infiltrated someone. He was a fink, a paid informer. We found out after he disappeared one day with our money and our files; all our neat schemes, forwarded to J. Edgar. I was ready to kill him, we both were, Shelby and I. I mean with a gun or a bomb. Ever been betrayed by someone you trusted? And he was someone I liked a lot, one of the best of the neat schemes was *his*, he was very bright and well educated, along with being on the payroll of the FBI. And he was a looker, too, Shelby was jealous. . . ."

I was tired of it. I looked out the window, the street was deserted now. There were only a few of us left in the restaurant. The empty street looked cold, lamplights glittered on dirty snow. I picked at my potato and realized I would have to go to the bank in the morning. She continued to talk, but I wasn't listening. I was thinking about money, how much I had spent and how much I had left. I said suddenly, "Where is he now?"

She paused fractionally, considering. "Vermont, as a matter of fact."

I nodded. It figured.

"South of here, somewhere near Rutland. He's living there with a group."

"Farming?"

"A little of this and a little of that."

I nodded sympathetically.

"It's a hard life," she said.

I nodded again. God knows she was right about that.

"But they're living in the way they choose, and judging from his letter, Shelby hasn't changed. He's still scheming and they're very much into wood stoves and foam insulation, and gardening."

Dope, I thought. Vermont's premier cash crop after fiddleheads and sweet corn. I looked out the window again, the two streetlights cast long, dark shadows. It really did look like one of Hopper's drypoint night scenes, except for the snow; Hopper worked with summers and autumns. It probably would have been better if we had met in the summer, the contrasts were not so great in summer. The days were long and the nights often warm, one or two nights a summer it was too warm for blankets. People took it easier in the summer; they were not so quick to judge. We were now at that point where every conversation turns into an argument. I found her past trivial, she found mine contemptible; and on that range, there was no room for maneuver. Of course the future was stubbornly opaque and we did not discuss it. I had let so much go in my life; this play would have to be hers.

The waiter came to collect our plates. He knew right away that we were at daggers drawn because he was correct and professional, no jokes. I ordered coffee and cognac for us both but Marty refused the cognac; she said she would continue with wine. When I turned back I saw her staring at me. She had her chin on the table and was staring at me through the Bordeaux. She drained it at a swallow and sat back in her chair, hands primly in her lap. I wondered if she were tight and decided that she was.

"You've made me up," she said, slowly and very distinctly. "I don't know who you think I am, but whoever it is, it's not *me*. And you don't want *me*. You want whoever it is you've made up. You're creating me as you go along, you're like Quinn and that creepy newspaperman he invented. Or worse: you're like a strip miner who sees the land only as something to be used for profit, yours. And who cares if you level the mountain or dig a hole half a mile deep, the land exists only for your benefit. Defoliate it, clear it, strip it, *occupy* it. *Break* it. Then you move on to some other territory and excavate that. I think you've done that with every woman you've ever known. You think we're property. And you think that we ought to be grateful, being given this great chance to yield what we have, allowing ourselves to be bought, invaded, conquered, and *used*. But tell me this. What do we get in return? What's our reward?"

"What do you know about the women I've known?"

"I can guess," she said.

"No, that's not something you're good at."

"And I don't even have to because you've told me. You've told me so much, more than you know. You've told me everything. And I remember because, just like you said, women have fucking good memories. You think we're mine fields. . . ." She went on like that, an inventory of things I had said, some in jest, some seriously. I felt reviled from the pulpit with secrets disclosed in the confessional.

"Boom boom," I said.

"They're women like me," she said. "They want to give but they want to hold on to something, too. Something of themselves. We aren't into white flags. We don't surrender, dear. And we don't want to give and give and give and give and not get one thing in return. *Nothing*."

"In exchange for all you've given," I said.

"Yes," she said.

"I'd call it an even exchange, nothing for nothing."

"You'd squeeze the blood out of a stone."

"And have," I said. "But you—"

"You think I've given nothing?"

"You don't like it, now that the game is almost over. It got serious and that was too much. Someone actually wanted to do something with the land besides look at it and ski on it. So things weren't so convenient anymore. Not quite so much *fun*. Not quite as loose as they were with the boy inventer and his sprinkler system and the savings bonds that a Rockefeller wouldn't quite buy. Jesus, Marty," I said. "Give me a break."

She picked up my snifter of cognac and slammed it down. She said, "You prick."

"It's a little more complicated than a downhill run, isn't it?"

"Prick."

"And I don't like it much, either, but at least I understand the stakes. The reward—what do you expect? What kind of 'reward' and for what—good behavior? Your reward's the same as mine, something shared, communicated, taken on faith. Being a shadow of each other. Your reward's me. My reward's you."

She looked away, out the window, down at her plate, over my shoulder, up at the ceiling, and out the window again. I thought she was crying but when she turned back to me her face was dry as granite. She seemed about to rise, then didn't.

"Did you hear any of that? Did you actually listen?"

"I heard it," she said.

"Believe any of it?"

"We come from different ends of the earth. I cannot believe what I heard. You are crazy."

160

◇

So we had run out of time, or perhaps it was only patience. I felt like an actor alone on an empty stage with no script and a full house growing restless and irritated. The stage was familiar—it seemed to me that I was always at a table in a restaurant, pouring the dregs of a bottle, the last to leave—but I had long since lost any vision of the last act. There was no escape, either. There could be no retreat to the beginning, there could only be an advance to the end— wherever it was. I had invested so much, and so had she. Our stage was littered with casualties, and it was unthinkable that they should have died in vain. I leaned across the table, wanting somehow to make it up. I did not want to think of us as enemies forever. It had been inconceivable to me that her passion was not the equal of mine. I had thought of it as an obvious physical principle: a clear sky makes possible a bright sun. The one did not exist without the other and it was not anything you could force or fabricate. I believed Marty was resisting for reasons of pride or school-girl confusion. In that way she resembled any emerging nation at odds with the momentous choices at hand, so numerous, so risky.

"It's not easy," I said.

She looked at me suspiciously, assuming that I was preparing another attack; but I had finished.

"You have so many choices."

She said, "Name one."

"Think of yourself politically. You could be Burma: close the gates to outsiders. Or you could be . . ." I tried to think of an attractive nation, one that would have the blessing of UNESCO or the editorial board of *The New York Times,* if not of the COMINTERN, that allowed substantial foreign investment and at the same time managed to keep control of its own destiny. Taiwan would not do, obviously. Or Chile or Poland, for the same reasons. "Mexico," I said.

She began to laugh.

"Canada," I amended.

161

Still laughing, she said, "What then?"

But I had another, more salient analogy. My mind was stacked with them like a baccarat shoe. I turned over a card and it said "Huckleberry Finn." Very well then, it would be Huck. I grinned. "We're in the great tradition, we're lighting out for the territory. We're leaving sullen civilization behind. It's like Huck Finn on the great river. The great river lies before us, rolling its mile-wide tide along. You and me, on de raf'."

"Which one's the nigger?" she asked.

I expanded on the theme. I gave it a passionate five minutes, then fell silent. I experienced a moment of vertigo, my frozen smile dissolving. "En here we is," I concluded lamely.

"That was some riff," she said. "Outstanding." I drank my coffee, coming back slowly from wherever I had been. She said, "You're wonderful when you're funny." She poured wine for us both, then—I believe she needed to share something, anything—took one of my cigarettes and waited while I lit it. She held it awkwardly and did not inhale. Marty was tight from the wine, tighter than I had ever seen her. When she began to speak she reached for my hand and held on. Twice she made me promise not to interrupt. I agreed to listen carefully, wanting so badly to hear what she had to say about us.

First place, she said, there were no empty places in her life. Nothing to justify and nothing to explain. No betrayals, she said seriously; no permanent loyalties, either, except to herself. "The past"—she looked away, calculating—"three or four years I've never been without someone great. Except for the past six months, until you. Needed those months because after Shelby I didn't need or want. Anyone. It was necessary to get beyond Shelby." She looked at me, smiling coyly. "Sometimes it takes a hell of a man to be better than no man at all. Things have been fine, except I've been confused about what I wanted to do with my life. . . ."

Well, I thought, I could give her expert testimony on

that. I lit a cigarette, losing concentration. I signaled for more coffee and watched the waiter while he poured two cups. Then I looked at her. She was rolling her wineglass with both hands, emphasizing the points she made. Her dark eyes were on the tablecloth, and across its width I smelled her scent, so provocative. She continued to talk, describing who she was and what she wanted from life. She was speaking slowly and clearly, but I could not concentrate on the words, they disappeared almost as soon as she spoke them.

". . . you," she said, "that first night. The things you said. The way we connected, it seemed so natural and friendly. . . ."

I tried to listen but couldn't. I was possessed now by an old blues and was trying to recall exactly how Yancey played it. My foot moved to my imagined music, and I thought then that she was probably right. I wasn't suited to live with anyone, I was narcissistic and too dissatisfied with things. Better to try living alone for a while. I tried to think of an agreeable place, perhaps the altiplano of Peru. Llamas, coca leaves, and the great height of the Andes beyond, the impenetrable culture of the Indians; it was a rarefied atmosphere, twelve thousand feet above sea level, close to God and Bolivia.

"I'm not *lacking*," she said. "Do you see what I'm saying?"

I nodded. I put the altiplano out of mind, and then I switched off Yancey. It was ridiculous, I had never lived alone in my life. I was incapable of living alone. I drank my coffee, listening. She spoke mechanically, one word after another. ". . . it's too complicated and I'm not talking only about the obvious conflicts. I have to have a clear run, that's the benefit of the times we live in, one of the unexpected results of your history. Yours and Quinn's. I'm entitled to it, I've thought a lot about myself and what will satisfy me and I know one thing for sure. I don't intend to be disappointed and I don't intend to spend my life forgiving people, men. Or myself, either. The other night you really got to me, I don't think you know how much—"

What night was that? She was talking more rapidly now, her face close to mine, with a burning intensity that enclosed and silenced me. Watching her was like watching a movie in a foreign language. I concentrated, but the sense of what she was saying eluded me. She assigned different meanings to familiar words. And she was implacable, though any casual observer in the restaurant would assume we were making love.

"—you said you didn't mind and wouldn't want to change my unreliability and I know you mean that, I'm sure you're sincere. Except you would. You couldn't help it. You'd take me over and suddenly the things that are simple would become complicated and I wouldn't know how to handle them because I wouldn't be *me*. So that leaves the last thing."

She pressed her finger on the glass face of her wristwatch, holding a minute, silent. Then she smiled, her mouth parting in a full grin. So happy, surely now she would say something extraordinary. But she turned away and giggled. "I feel like one of the early scientists, a wizard or sorceress or magician."

She said, "All this, I can't bear to lose it. You, us here together, our friendship, what we mean to each other." Then she was quiet a moment. She took another cigarette from the package on the table, and I leaned forward to light it; but she put it down. Her movie commenced to roll again. "So I was thinking of the way I want it to be," she said. The picture was vivid in her mind and as she began to describe it in detail her voice became gentler, almost musical. She leaned back in her chair, obviously charmed by her own vision of the spacious future. It was this. She would return to her mountain and I to mine. In the mornings when the sun was just rising and the snow unbroken we would think of each other, our best selves. Then we would go to work, she on her trail and I on mine. Was it not so that we were both working last chapters of a particular book? It was necessary to get beyond this chapter in order to begin the next volume. And what a volume it would be! There were no limits to what we might achieve, if we kept faith with each other. I can be what you want me to be, she said; I can be that at a distance. From time to time we would meet for a meal, and exchange our news. I had so much to tell her, my life had been crowded and fraught; my experience, shared with her, would acquire a new life. And she had much to share with me as well, not experience—not fact, not episode—but *faith*. Only that.

Oh, she said, her eyes shining. We'll have a great success, you and I. Your ship's out of the bottle and running at flank speed. Mine, too. We'll support and cherish each other, great friends always. Her hands were together, folded on the table. She said, "That's the way I want it to be." But we had to struggle for it and be tough about it. We had to be tough as terrorists. Nothing came cheap. "And I can feel it going sour," she said.

I said quietly, "But you can't have it both ways."

She looked at me blankly. "Why not?"

I said, "No one can."

"But of course you can!" She stared at me, astonished, as if while we were levitating I'd informed her of the law of gravity.

I paused then and turned away. At the bar in the corner the waiter was reading the racing form. The other diners had left and there were just Marty and me at table. I thought of the slender woman, my wife's friend, and her husband, wondering where they were now; well, they would be in bed. The waiter looked at me and raised an eyebrow. I winked at him, then returned to the situation. Marty's vision of the spacious future stayed with me, but so did her question. She couldn't know what she was proposing. "Because you have to make choices," I said.

"Who says so?"

Who says so? I do. Everybody says so. It's a law.

She bent toward me, her eyes dark and settled. She

was not at all tight now. She pushed a lock of hair away from her forehead and smiled condescendingly. "It's not good enough," she said. "It won't go the way you want it to go. You want too much. You want everything there is and nothing goes that way anymore. Your experience, my faith; and faith's stronger."

I did not know exactly what she meant by faith. She did not seem to mean loyalty. It was probably simple belief. "You and I . . ." I began but did not finish the sentence. She waited but I had forgotten what it was I wanted to say.

"Don't ruin it," she said.

"I don't want to ruin it," I said.

"I feel bad about myself," she said suddenly. "And I don't like that. That isn't the way I like to feel."

"My fault," I said.

"Yes," she agreed.

I stared at her a full minute. Perhaps if I put it in her vernacular. "I don't want it as heavy as you think I do." This was a lie.

And she knew it. "Yes, you do. You want it as heavy as you can get it, the heavier the better, because you thrive on it. You like long twilight struggles, they're attractive to you. You think it's romantic. You think it's cool. You want to civilize the savages. You think you're *heroic*. The only battle that counts is the last one, right?" Satisfied, she nodded once, curtly, her eyes hard and far away. Her movie had ended.

I tossed off the last of my cognac and thought about withdrawal, an orderly retirement. Perhaps the wilderness was not so feral as I imagined, or my own resources so meager. And if it was twilight, who could say with certainty that the coming darkness was not benevolent? As for this experience, surely she was the stronger for it; as, most certainly, was I. I was protecting my own future now, though I knew that whatever I said or did the bill was already reckoned. I explained all this in detail, and when I finished she turned away, fighting an impulse to weep—or to laugh—I wasn't sure which. In the end she did neither and we sat silently watching each other. My friend the waiter was dozing now over the racing form. She was wary, her body coiled tight as a spring. Had I truly withdrawn, or merely executed a feint?

She said, "Did you like your dinner?"

"The shrimp was tops," I said. "The rest of it was routine. But we did well on the wine, three bottles."

"That many? You drank most of it."

We waited quietly and then I began to talk about my book, which turned into a description of my life, the quotidian, the good mornings as well as the bad. I wanted everything on the record, no concealed evidence. I described my house in the mountains and how it settled in the shank of the seasons, the woods dark and still, the air cold or turning cold, the sky gray as lead. It was hard for me to remember the specifics of the good weather. The north country was particular, wasn't it? It was all right to go back to basics in the woods, but we were more remote than necessary; we were thrown back on our own resources exclusively. I smiled. There were no decent restaurants in the north country, I said. All we had were STEAKS CHOPS SEAFOOD COCKTAILS.

I enjoyed duck hunting on an isolated lake near the border with an old acquaintance, a retired soldier; he was an older man who had known Stalin, the tyrant easy to comprehend in these surroundings, so reminiscent of Mother Russia, the birches and great forests and the cold; this part of the country was virgin virtually to the Arctic Circle. But when I tried to retail the soldier's anecdotes to my wife she refused to listen; the anecdotes were subtle but savage in their description of Stalin's evil.

Once I took my son into the woods back of the house, looking for grouse or woodcock. But he was frightened of the shotgun and didn't like the idea of killing birds. I had wanted nothing more than to go hunting with my father when I was a boy. My father was an excellent shot. They

167

would've gotten on well, Marty's father and mine. I described my study, the photographs and the souvenirs, and my old manual typewriter and the woman who came in to clean, and the woman's erratic personal life. She was a marvelous woman and a hard worker but her personal life was turbulent. She took it in good stride, though, explaining that north-country life was demanding and the key to it was maintenance. Use it up, wear it out, make it do, or do without. To this disjointed monologue, Marty had nothing whatever to say.

I finished my coffee, cold now, and paid the bill, a hundred and fifty dollars. I counted the money out and my friend the waiter made change at the table. I left a forty-dollar tip for the inconvenience. I had started the week with five hundred dollars and now I had only fifty in my wallet. Marty commented on the size of the bill, taking another cigarette from the package on the table; then she put it down. She said that I encouraged all her bad habits—smoking, eating too much, drinking every night, staying up late. She was supposed to be in training. She picked up the cigarette and snapped it in two.

"You," she said softly. She faced me now across the table, her dark hair falling to the cloth. She did not look like a wizard or sorceress now, only an American college girl. I was leaning away from her, arms loose at the sides of my body; small change lay in the waiter's dish between us. She stated, "So you know exactly how I feel. I could be what you want me to be. That's exactly what scares me, you want to know the truth. I'm positive I could be that, I know exactly what you want." She looked at me solemnly, the words coming now in single shots. "To be that to somebody, it's a great thing, really tremendous. And I could be that for you, just what you want. But—" She lifted her arms helplessly and let them fall. "It wouldn't be right. And you'd owe me."

I nodded and moved the waiter's tray a fraction. The starved candle was throwing a vagrant light. Whatever could

168

she mean? How much would I owe her? And what were the terms? Our eyes met and held. At last she was vulnerable, leaning toward me now, awaiting my reply. One swift thrust, I thought, and I could occupy her country again. But the moment was gone almost as soon as it arrived. Perhaps she was right after all and I was hopelessly attracted to twilight. But the trump was not there when I needed it, so I only smiled and nodded, and when I spoke it was to give reassurance only. "Peace is at hand," I said.

◇

We left the restaurant and walked slowly back to the hotel, through streets glittering with snow. It was very cold but the town was cozy, so late at night. It was a pretty little town and I liked it. I took her arm and we turned into the hotel's narrow street with its low, two-story wooden buildings. The street had an old-fashioned western look to it. I couldn't imagine how we had ever arrived here, this place, from our separate starting points.

The dull lights of the marquee were in front of us. We walked very slowly now, not speaking, our boots squeaking on the snow. We passed a dour little bar with young men inside, pressed together in the glare of the television set. They were local men, the tourists were all in bed. They were watching the news, of course, an official standing in front of a government building, or perhaps it was a correspondent, often it was hard to tell them apart. The white-aproned owner was behind the bar, holding a bottle of Bud. No doubt the man on the screen was talking politics. No one at the bar was talking. We paused briefly, looking through the misty window into the interior; then we hurried on. In the foyer of the hotel she turned to say something, but I touched her arm and shook my head.

Yet upstairs in the room I was unable to end it. She tilted her head sadly and lifted her face to be kissed, then aggressively embraced me. We stood in the darkness a very long time and she began to cry, the tears welling, then falling. She made no sound, leaning against me, her fists tight on my chest.

Then her arms were at her side, and after a final murmured sentence she moved away and began to brush her hair, a few short businesslike strokes. Until the last minute I was certain she'd nod her head or look at me and smile or otherwise indicate that I was to join her. But she climbed into bed alone and hung there on its edge, like a lip of snow on a roof. I watched her from the window and in five minutes her expression softened, freezing, and she was asleep.

ten

I drove her to the base lodge in the morning, early. A few instructors were about, waxing skis and doing their warmups. She was full of nervous chatter about improvements at Stowe. The owners were putting two million dollars into Spruce Peak and everyone was pleased that *Playboy* had rated the mountain "Best in the East" for nightlife. It was like winning an Oscar. A mountain had an image, just like a movie star or TV entertainer, and Stowe's was changing from "family" to "single," or "swingle," as the older ones liked to style themselves. They were the ones who read *Playboy*.

"Do you know what they say to you when they want you to spend the night with them?"

I shook my head. I hadn't the faintest idea.

"They say, 'Let's have breakfast together.' "

How droll, I thought. I said, "I'll be a son of a gun."

Playboy attracted big spenders. It was a shame that so many of them were assholes, but that was not her concern. Capitalism was thriving in Vermont, where Stowe and Sugarbush competed as viciously as Detroit and Osaka. There was a wonderful Ph.D. thesis to be done on the Vermont economy, so peculiar. In some ways it was like the Costa Brava, except that instead of the profits expatriated to Hamburg or Geneva they were expatriated to Boston and New York. Really, Stowe had an international clientele. Last week she had given private lessons to a Japanese family, a woman and her husband and their two sons. They were a nice family, polite and attentive, and eager to learn. The husband carried a video camera to record his family's progress on the slopes. They were not very adept, however. And he didn't tip worth a damn.

Well, she said.

We were sitting in the car, keeping warm. I rolled down the window to throw out my cigarette. The sky was dark with low clouds and it was hard to know what time it was. I guessed it was just after eight. There were already a few skiers on the slopes. We got out of the car and stood a moment in the cold. Skiers were trooping up the walk in twos and threes, their amiable chatter filling the silence between Marty and me. She did a deep knee bend, then checked to see that she had all her gear. Someone said hello to her and she nodded, distracted.

Okay, she said.

I told her to keep well.

She told me to take care.

I told her to watch out for playboys offering breakfast.

She said, Don't be mean.

I said, I'm joking.

She touched my forehead and made a face. She said, Take care of that head.

I said I would.

We kissed lightly, once, and she moved off up the walk to the base lodge. An instructor intercepted her and they stood and chatted a moment. I heard a guitar, country music, "Whiskey River." It was the boy in the red parka, and after they had spoken he turned around to look at me. He waved and I waved back. I was turning to get back into the car when I heard her call my name. She took a step forward and tilted her head, raising her chin; and with her right hand made a show of catching a champagne flute falling

172

from the crown of her head. The boy in the red parka smiled, enjoying the pantomime.

I got into my car and drove off, back down the mountain road through the Stowe chalet country. There was a steady stream of cars heading the other way, in the direction of the slopes—Goat, Nosedive, and the others. In the village I visited the pharmacy to buy a bottle of aspirin, the Montpelier newspaper, and yesterday's *New York Times*. I took the papers and the aspirin and returned to the hotel, hoping that the dour little tavern down the street was open. Surprisingly, it was. There was only one other customer, and the bartender was watching the *Today* show. I installed myself at the quiet end of the bar and ordered coffee and cognac to go with the coffee, and a glass of water for the aspirin. It had been almost a week since I'd read a newspaper and I read these thoroughly, starting with the sports and working backward. The Patriots were losing, Liz Taylor was in the hospital with an undisclosed ailment, the House was debating the defense budget, and the weather was expected to remain the same. There was nothing about the boat people.

"No downhill run today?"

The question came from the customer at the other end of the bar. He gave me a short salute and I recognized the gray-haired skier with the silver flask and the West Point ring. He had been there all this time. He heaved himself off the bar stool, his heavy leather boots crashing on the wood floor. I put my papers aside and walked down the bar. The bartender watched us curiously as we shook hands. I asked him if I could buy him a drink and he shook his head; he was on his way out, back to the slopes. He had a regime, fifteen runs a day, more if he could manage it. I could believe this, he looked fit and cheerful.

I said, "Thanks a hell of a lot for the other day."

He laughed. "You took a fine fall. Outstanding."

"Well, I appreciate it. And the whiskey, too." He smiled and tapped his rear pocket, *clunk clunk:* the flask. I knew that I would have to be the first to ask, so I said, "When were you there?"

"Sixty-four," he said, "and again in sixty-eight." He reached behind him for his scarf and cap and sweater. The scarf was neatly folded beside an empty snifter and a half-empty carafe of coffee. The sweater was wool, olive drab with patches on the elbows.

I wanted to ask him which units he had served with, and where. In the war we were all tight with each other, everyone was a friend or a friend of a friend; in the war he would have been a captain or major. No question, we had mutual friends. He put a bill on the bar, then pulled on his sweater and wrapped the scarf around his neck. I said instead, "I was there in the middle of your tours. I left before sixty-eight, when everything went to hell."

He nodded without apparent interest, put on his gloves, and walked away toward the door. I noticed his boots, polished to a high shine—Corcorans, the boot of choice of the airborne. He turned toward me when he opened the door and I saw that he was laughing, a soundless laugh but full of—it looked like scorn. He was shaking his head. "God," he said, and laughed out loud. "Wasn't it a son of a bitch?" Then, still laughing, he closed the door and was gone.

I stayed in the bar for an hour and a half. The papers, read and reread, turned out to be four cognacs long. When I finished, I returned to the hotel and checked out. Then I went to the bank and cashed a check. The teller, hesitating, looked at me queerly and asked me if I was all right. I had broken into a sweat and had trouble controlling my fingers. I said that I thought I was coming down with the flu, and the teller nodded sympathetically; it was going around.

I started driving again, not knowing exactly where I was going. The roads all looked the same, and the sky was so dark I could not make out the direction; it was all one direction. I picked up a hitchhiker but she wanted out after a mile or two. I had asked her where I was going, and she had misinterpreted; I only wanted to know the direction, the point on the compass. It was confusing to me, this gray country. I could go home or return to Quinn's or drive south to Boston or New York or Washington, but in this part of the world the roads wound this way and that, and the villages were unfamiliar. I did not recognize any of them.

I stopped for gas and bought a road map and abruptly decided to return to Quinn's. I had not seen either him or Tessa for days, it seemed. Quinn's was the one friendly place I knew. I drove north, stopping for a late lunch, a cheeseburger and two beers and more coffee and cognac. I read the Burlington newspaper and the current edition of *Time*. I was steady and no longer sweating. The cognac had no effect at all.

◇

I arrived at Quinn's in the late afternoon. The Land-Rover was gone, Quinn having taken it to town on an errand. Tessa embraced me in the doorway. She was enthusiastic and cheerful, then unaccountably nervous. She said I looked all in, helping me with my coat and suggesting a nap. But I insisted I was fine. I was eager to talk, to get everything off my mind. We sat at opposite ends of the couch. She was staring at me intently and did not seem to mind when I touched her knee or her hand to emphasize a particular part of the narrative; it comforted me to touch her. In the beginning, Tessa interrupted me often to ask clarifying questions; she seemed confused by the story. After a while she just sat quietly and listened. I had trouble with the chronology, and the last night with Marty was a blur. I realized I was telling the story as if it had happened to someone else; it was a secondhand story that I had heard somewhere. I wanted to make it arresting and added a humorous touch here and there; but Tessa was not amused.

She made coffee, which I corrected with cognac.

She said that wasn't such a good idea.

I said maybe not, but it was the only one I had.

When I finished telling the story, or as much of it as

I could assemble, Tessa turned away and I saw she was crying.

I leaned toward her. What was wrong?

She looked at me with her beautiful wet face. Her look was one of desolation, conceivably anger. She started to say something, then shook her head as if words were no use in this matter. She sighed finally and said, "Oh, God."

I felt a surge of feeling and moved toward her. But she was up and turning on the lights. We had been sitting in near darkness. I said something about it being better to curse the candles and she smiled bleakly. She put the palms of her hands into her eyes and worked them back and forth. I wanted so badly to be close to her. I said, "You are so pretty."

She turned toward me with an affectionate look; or perhaps it was only pity. I knew it was the sort of look you give someone who misses the point of the joke. She said, "Thank you."

I was at sea. I did not understand why she was crying, or why she was angry at me, and said so.

Tessa stared at me a long moment, her eyes widening; her hands were on her cheeks. "I'm not mad at you," she said slowly, and then, her voice rising, "I'm not *mad*. Why should I be *mad*? We've all had such a lovely time. It's been so jolly, so much good cheer. Hasn't it been *super*? Hasn't it been *just ducky*. God, mad." She was crying again. "How could I possibly be *mad*. None of this has anything to do with me, has it? I'm the innocent bystander, aren't I? Doesn't anybody. Don't any of you *men*"—she bit off the word—"have any sense at all of the value of things? The value of peace, which only means the absence of disorder. You people." She raised her hands, then let them fall, the universal gesture of helplessness. "You're too complicated for me, maybe that's it."

"No," I said.

"Yes, that's right," she said harshly. "Me too, I'm a part of it." She looked away, then back at me, her eyes pleading. I was watching her every movement, thinking that somewhere there would be a clue. She seemed to be punishing herself. I rose to go to her but she made a little gesture and moved to the fireplace and stood there alone, her back to me. She said, "I have a friend in London. I'm fonder of her than anyone, she has two little girls. I don't see as much of her as I'd like because she and her husband and the girls are always off somewhere, they spend their weekends together as a family in the country picnicking and driving here and there. She's so much fun to be with, she's a person who makes you feel good when she walks into a room. And the girls are cute, they're a real family. And about a year ago I held my breath. My friend's husband . . ." She paused, and seemed to consider; she did not complete the sentence. She said, "But he *didn't*. He chose not to. His choice. And they're still together, and I want to believe they'll be together always, and I don't." She raised her head and looked directly at me. "We're all understrength."

It was dark outside. The windows reflected the interior in wavy shapes, Tessa standing, me sitting, the lamps, the coffee table. I watched her move suddenly, undulating in the glass.

She said, "No one wanted this. I didn't. Quinn didn't."

"I did," I said.

"No, you didn't." She stated this as a simple truth. "Why don't you go to bed."

But it was too late for that. I began to wind back in my memory. Where had this begun? I tried to picture Tessa's friend and the two cute girls and the friend's husband who chose not to. He was the sort of man who had clear sight, who could see disaster coming a mile away. He would heed those who said, It's unwinnable. Get out of it. Go home. Go back to your wife and kids.

I said, "It's what happens when you get lost in the last chapter."

She shook her head firmly. No sale.

177

And no wonder. The retreat into work was a safe port in any storm. One had a mission in life and this mission was sacrosanct, and a justification for any aggression. I said, "And it's still there, the manuscript's on the dresser. I take it everywhere, along with my notebooks and Buddha. Max Beckmann's guarding them." She wasn't listening. She put her hand over her eyes, then took it away and stood up straight. I liked her greatly, but knew better than to move toward her again. I said, "Don't worry, please. I can straighten all this out. In a year it'll be forgotten."

She said, "It better not be."

When she had turned on the lights, I noticed a naked Christmas tree in the corner. I rose unsteadily and went to it. It had always been fun, decorating the Christmas tree. We decorated it on the twentieth and took it down on New Year's Day and fed it piece by piece into the fire, the tinsel curling as if it were alive. Tessa watched me a moment, then pushed herself away from the mantel, like a battered fighter answering the bell. She said that she and Quinn had bought the tree at the supermarket the day before but had not gotten around to decorating it.

The tree looked odd, plain.

Yes, she agreed.

I asked her why they had bought a tree at the supermarket when there was a forest of them surrounding the house.

She shook her head. She didn't know. It was Quinn's idea. She hooked her arm through mine and we walked into the kitchen. She prepared tea for us both and told me of the past few days with Quinn, hard times in the north country. Quinn was not communicative and she had never felt more a passenger. She described him in the early mornings, bent over the piano; it seemed to her that he was always at the piano playing the blues or at his desk writing. She said that she knew now that she would have to return home, where-ever that was, her flat or her mother's house or her father's place. She guessed it was her own flat. She wanted to be home in London, its familiar smell and ambience, its enormity. She wanted her flat in Covent Garden, where there were no pianos and the cognac was always at full strength. We were back in the living room, looking at the Christmas tree. She handed me my teacup and we both smiled, understanding that we were guests in another man's house, singular terrain that wasn't home for her any more than it was for me.

She said, "Where will you go now?"

But I had no answer to that question.

We stood beside the Christmas tree, a scrawny, desiccated thing; in my house we wouldn't give it a second look. She described the hilarious excursion to the shopping mall— Quinn insisted on pronouncing it "mal" to rhyme with "pal"— then held out her wrist and shook it. A gold bangle danced there, Quinn's impulsive Christmas present, the most expensive piece in the store. They had gotten it the day before yesterday. It was snowing and Quinn with his stomach and beard looked like Father Christmas, or a dissipated Santy Claus. The excursion was fun and he was sweet and affectionate when he gave her the bangle, and for a time she thought it would be all right. She looked at me.

"You and the kid were gone and we were alone for a change."

But the house was haunted, she said. The ghosts were everywhere. Perhaps Quinn was haunted, too. He talked on and on about his books, the blues, and Marty, but nothing was resolved and it became tiresome, listening to a monologue. He didn't care whether she listened or not, he only wanted an audience. "The way men do," she said.

In retrospect, she said, perhaps it was her fault. She had not demanded enough or had demanded the wrong things. She was a victim, but often a victim is an accomplice; let a court sort it out. More likely, she and Quinn were not suited. She had not seen him clearly and as her mother had warned, the Americans were very queer these days. As Quinn moved farther into himself, she backed away. Who wouldn't?

She didn't know what he was looking for. She didn't know what he wanted from her.

"You have to know that," she said, turning to look at me; I avoided her eyes. "That is the one thing you have to know. It's more than simply *wanting*. You have to know why, and what. I mean you." She touched my arm. "You have to know that."

And one thing was obvious, she should have known it from the beginning. It was her error, hers alone. It was always a mistake to draw power from another's circuit.

Ness pa?

I smiled.

"That's better," she said. "End of lecture." She began to reminisce, recalling the first night we'd met, at the party, and, later, Marty and me tête-à-tête on the stairs. She asked me what we were talking about sitting in the dark stairwell so still and close, and I thought and thought but couldn't remember. It was a dazzling conversation, though. My arrival at Quinn's and all that followed seemed to us both a thousand years ago, an episode from our dark ages; the roots of our little civilization, which had flourished so brilliantly for a while.

Up to a point, she said.

And we know so little about each other really. We had always been surrounded by noise and activity. We were supporting players at the opera; and it was our opera. She thought it incredible that we had never talked seriously. I had never described to her my life in the north country, and what had driven me to Quinn's. She was a mystery to me as I was a mystery to her. We knew each other as houseguests, without lives of our own, or rules, or other loyalties.

She said, "It's a relief, being finished with Quinn. He's exhausting."

I smiled at her. "He's too old for you."

She smiled back. "No, he isn't. But that's another story. In the beginning we were great for each other, except we speak in different voices. He understood mine better than

180

I understood his. And no wonder, I was kind of lost. Now I'm found again. And I know what I'm going to do. I'm going back to Britain and I'm going back to work." She considered that a moment, sipping her tea. "Quinn never liked my little flat. He was there, just once. I think we were picking up some of my things. He didn't like its location and he didn't like the clutter. Because of the clutter, he didn't think I was serious about my work. That's the truth."

I was suddenly restless, unable to be still. I had moved from the fireplace to the window and back again, listening to her. I thought it was important to keep moving. I had an image of being pursued, run to ground by the events of the past three days. If I kept moving, they could not find me. I said, "Let's get out of here. Right away. Let's go to Boston."

"What about him?"

"We'll leave Quinn a note. Tell him to fly down and meet us at the Ritz bar."

She looked at me and shook her head. It was not hard to read my mind, and she was no understudy or surrogate. I did not press it. The cognac was wearing off and I had a headache.

Then Quinn burst through the door. He was in a bois- terous mood, setting down a large parcel, kissing Tessa, slapping me on the back, booming instructions, and laying plans for the evening. He produced two envelopes from his coat pocket, the envelopes covered with writing in a micro- scopic hand. A highly successful afternoon in the gallery of the Vermont House, he said, the level of debate not quite up to the Commons but risible in its way; material enough for a trilogy, in fact. He began an involved story concerning his friend the lieutenant governor and Tory back-benchers, a dispute having to do with the state's relations with Canada . . .

"Republicans, Quinn," I said. "In America we call them Republicans."

Anyway, he went on, it was a whale of a debate. It was

outstanding. One of the Tories was a farmer who kept waving his left hand, a hand with only three fingers. The third finger was missing. This fascinated Quinn, he wondered how a man could lose the third finger; it would be quite a trick. So after adjournment he asked him. Quinn represented himself as a visiting journalist and asked him how he had come to lose his third finger, left hand. Damn fool thing, the legislator said. He'd been a farmer all his life and one day he was fixing the thresher and not paying attention and a piece of machinery caught his wedding ring and snapped his finger right off, like so. There are three or four of us in this place, he said, missing fingers. Makes you wonder about wearing a wedding ring, he said, but what the hell. I know another guy, thresher got him by the *belt*, boy jeezum.

God, he said, it was a great day. A hell of a day. Quinn examined me closely, as a physician might, and inquired after my health. Fine, I said. Excellent, Quinn replied. He clapped his hands, he had a surprise. Then he looked at me again. "What did she do, hit you?" He reached out to touch my tender forehead, and I backed away.

I said, "A brawl."

He laughed. Well then, a good thing, his surprise. In Montpelier he was not only interrogating Tories. He had visited the gourmet food shop. He opened the parcel and brought out wheels of cheese, a wedge of pâté, smoked salmon, Virginia ham, and various tins—smoked oysters, sardines, Japanese shrimp, black olives, and artichoke hearts. There was plenty of champagne in the basement. He turned to me, cocking an eyebrow. Shall we set the table for three or four? he asked. I said, Three, and he nodded briskly and launched into a fresh anecdote about a fairy who tried to pick him up in the gourmet food shop.

I excused myself to take a shower. Quinn's energy demanded so much. I could not focus my eyes and I was sweating, no coherence anywhere. I wished I had gone to Boston with Tessa. I did not want to eat exotic food or drink champagne. I showered quickly, after pouring a cognac. When I finished, I poured another cognac. I looked at myself in the mirror, wondering if I looked as ruined as I felt. I did not recognize the man in the tuxedo. I hefted my manuscript, thinking that I had put so much of myself into it that there was nothing left over; there were no reserves. But wasn't that what you were supposed to do, wring yourself out, give everything that you had? What was the point of it, if you were unwilling to risk everything? I knew then that I did not exist beyond the war. I was a creature of it. And I could not end it. I could not *conclude* it. I wondered if it had no conclusion; perhaps it would go on and on, living as long as I did. No: everything has an end. Love does. Life does. War does. If there is a beginning, there has to be an end, though modern physics would contradict that theory. To hell with modern physics. To hell with Marty. To hell with Quinn. I wheeled and threw my glass at Max Beckmann, hitting him squarely in the mouth; the glass shattered and flew around the room, it seemed to me in slow motion, the glass floating, sharp, dangerous, pretty in the rosy light from the lamp.

When I moved back down the stairs to the kitchen I saw them in the living room, Quinn shaking his head. His voice was strident. He didn't want to hear about it. It hadn't worked, as he knew it wouldn't; as any damned fool knew it wouldn't, and a good thing. She knew her own mind, in that way she was a model young American woman. As for me, I would survive; I always had. In any case, he did not want to hear the details, one look at my face told him all he needed to know. He knew the facts already. "I know what they are without hearing them from you," he said.

"Quinn, it's a sad story and he's really shot—"

"No doubt. It's always a sad story."

"It's the saddest story I ever heard," she said defiantly.

"I doubt that," Quinn said. "What does she say about it?"

"She called," Tessa said. I cupped my hand to my ear

and leaned forward, not wanting to miss this news. "She feels badly but he left her no choice. He was asking for it, she said."

"Boo-hoo," Quinn said. "Just tell me one thing, as if I didn't know the answer already. Does he figure it was worth it, his escapade? Any regrets?"

"Yes to the first," she said. "And yes to the second."

"God," he said, "it's too comical."

It was all far away, nothing to do with me, this description of a battle between two obscure armies in a remote Third World country. I listened to it as if I were a reporter eavesdropping on a conversation between two government officials. At any moment I expected the salient fact to fall, the missing piece to my puzzle.

Quinn said, "He wanted a new life. I wonder if he likes it, now that he has it."

His cold superiority finally reached her, for when she spoke her voice fluttered. She said, "You're a bastard sometimes."

He grunted, no argument.

"You're pathetic."

"Ha."

"Bastard."

"Go ahead. One more."

"Second-rater. Lightweight."

"I am not here to tell lies," Quinn said.

I watched her turn away and move to the window. She stood looking into the darkness. She dried her eyes and leaned against the glass, slumping with exhaustion. Quinn came up silently behind her and put his hands on her shoulders.

She shrugged, avoiding him.

"I'm sorry." He put his arm around her. "Don't call me second-rate, though."

"You're too rough," she said.

"I know it. But that doesn't make me second-rate."

"You hurt people."

"Know that, too."

"You hurt me."

"Sorry again. I don't want to hurt you. But I see things in my own way, and won't lie about it."

"Do you know something?" she said after a moment. "I'm feeling nostalgic for my flat, my own things. The greengrocer on the corner, the pub down the street. The theater, my friends. There was a painting I was working on, and now I can hardly remember what it was, and what I wanted it to be. This place is so distant. You're so distant. I want to go home."

"Do you want to go now?"

"After Christmas," she said. "We can have Christmas here, but I want to do it my way. Decorate the Christmas tree. Have a Christmas goose and a pudding, and stockings over the fireplace. Is there somewhere we can go to midnight mass? I suppose not. Christmas isn't so bad," she said, smiling bleakly. "Give Christmas a chance."

"I never liked your flat," he said.

She turned away. "I know."

"Why do you suppose I never liked it?"

"Because it was mine," she said.

◇

A man who danced to his own blues. He could not lie, I could not find the truth. His life, so solitary on the inside and so crowded without; mine, the reverse. I poured another cognac and took it upstairs. I intended to change my shirt, but once in the room forgot why I was there. I looked at the freshly made bed and walked into the bathroom, scene of my midnight deliberations. I could never walk into this bedroom without thinking of us together, what we did and what we said, the confidence with which we began and the way we petered out, grasping at straws. We had not had the will to see it through, and victory was so close. We were not suited, it was true; but that was only an accident of history. There was a way to make it good, I was certain of

185

that. We had invested so much, and there was ever so much worth saving.

I stayed only a moment, then returned to the living room. All the lights were on but it was empty. Quinn and Tessa were in the kitchen. I heard murmuring, a low, intimate sibilance, and private laughter. I looked hard at the barren Christmas tree, then at the inviting darkness outside. Quinn's drink was on the coffee table, untouched. I finished mine and took his and went to the wetroom. I put on my boots and down vest and shell and took my hat and gloves and left the house without a word, Quinn's drink cold in the pocket of my vest.

I had it in mind that I would visit the place where we had lunched on the red tablecloth. I followed our path up the old logging road, a faint white blur in the darkness. Last week's tracks were still visible, two parallel lines, a kind of pentimento in the snow. There was no light anywhere so I lit a cigarette. I looked back down the road but the lights of Quinn's house had vanished. There were no stars anywhere, and no wind. I was saving the drink for the moment I arrived, because I believed she would be there. I thought she was there now. The closer I got to our place the more elated I became, certain that this breach between us was the result of a simple misunderstanding. She knew how serious it was with me, and how much I was prepared to risk.

But when I arrived I was alone.

I called her name, believing she would suddenly appear, on the trail or from behind one of the great firs. But there was nothing at all, not with the first shout or the second or the third. I listened for echoes, but there were none. I leaned into the silence, waiting, my mind heaving; then I was at one with the silence.

I walked back down the trail. It was possible that she was searching for me as I was searching for her, and even now she was following my tracks. Of course that would have to be it, but it was dangerous for her, an attractive

186

young woman alone late at night in the Green Mountains. I loitered for a moment, calling her name. I finished the last of Quinn's drink, and threw the glass as far as I could; when it landed, it made no sound. Farther along, I lit another cigarette, watching the windows of Quinn's house. The yellow light was inviting, and there was movement inside. I closed my eyes against the cold, and when I opened them she was there, circling on the margins of my vision. I watched her curve toward me. I dropped my cigarette and did not move, not wanting to spook her. If she saw me she'd flare for sure, disappearing into the night sky, lifting away forever. The hat obscured her face. She turned to the man with her and he nodded, taking her arm. They passed nearby, talking so softly I heard nothing; I noticed only the bobbing of their heads. The man was talking earnestly at her, his hand on her waist. She shook her head gravely at something he said and put her arms around his neck. It was a gesture of the most open affection. They clung, swaying, holding a moment; then she kissed him on the mouth. They seemed to kiss for a very long time, the two of them slender and blurred in the light from Quinn's house. I closed my eyes, grieved at this tableau. And when I opened them again, they were gone, Marty and her anonymous escort.

I moved to where they had stood. Her light scent still held in the cold dry air, and I stood silent, surrounded by it, dazed, moving backward and forward in time. The light was bright and hurt my eyes. The light was lurid in this clear air. I leaned against a maple tree, observing the vicinity through two sets of eyes, in equal balance and opposed to each other, at once holding on and letting go. Heeling to one side and then another, I determined that the seas were heavy here. The place was as menacing and featureless as any ocean. I moved along, feeling myself slipping, my mind turning irresistibly on its axis, a ship swinging at anchor. Weary and morose, I gave way to the storm like single-handed Slocum at the helm of *Spray*, driving before heavy weather. This was the heaviest I'd seen, a mountainous heaving, the night white with blown spume, and cold as a corpse. My mind swung again, and I realized that I was sweating and that somehow between here and there I'd removed my glasses and put them in my pocket.

Quinn's house. I stood in the driveway looking in. The lights were on and there were people in the living room. A party was in progress. Quinn stood at the fireplace, telling a story, and his guests were laughing. Turning to my left, I waited for her. I saw my erratic footsteps in the snow and presently she was there beside me in her ulster and fedora, poker-faced. We did not touch but stood together, waiting for something to happen. Quinn turned to Tessa and put his arm affectionately around her. She smiled up at him, as women do in romantic films. All this was very clear. Marty jerked her fedora down over one eye and looked at me, grinning; really, she had a winning smile. She began to talk then, a low, serious monologue, very bitter, almost savage in its condemnation. She talked to me a long while in her sharp staccato voice and, listening to her, I knew that I would remember her accentless speech long after I had forgotten her face. Faces were the first features lost to memory, though my skull was crowded with them, faces reflecting every age, nationality, and human condition. They set up a swooning in my mind but when I looked away, they vanished; and when I turned back, she was gone. I was alone in the cold, stricken and distraught, drunk.

I looked up into the window of Quinn's house, watching the people who had appeared again in his living room; these were different from those inside my skuil, such a multitude of souls. I saw Willard Lopez, Roy Wendnagle, the lieutenant governor and his wife, and Betsy Dane talking to a handsome man with a lined face, whom I took to be the famous correspondent. He was most dashing. The bar was busy, Swig Borowy acting as barman. Quinn played the piano, the blue notes metallic in the cold. I saw it all, bright and cheerful, and as riotous as it had been on that first confused night. The future opened to me, a long and

happy life at Quinn's house in an atmosphere of truce, far
from the war—how mournful it had been, I thought, to
witness a campaign not merely wrong but incomprehen-
sible. Then I moved to the front step, Marty on my arm.
Intimate again, we shared a sexual glow. I smiled hopefully.
She would be the catalyst in that room, a provocateur sure
enough for those of us who had been left behind on the field
of fire. I hesitated, perhaps she did not belong after all;
perhaps it would be better if she did not know how easily
things broke. And no doubt it was better that we not be
reminded, if the truce were to endure.

She shivered and suddenly I feared for her future, in
this time so dark with disorder and gathering panic. We
had turned the past upside down and were without consolation. I moved toward her. It was necessary that she understand this and make her own choice. She was there and
then she wasn't and for an instant another vision formed
in my mind, expiring almost as it appeared: I was standing
alone in a little clearing, scrutinizing a landlocked blue-
green valley bounded by forested mountains rising in mist,
pastoral, inviting, innocent, unapproachable, trackless, cold,
far from home.

With that, I opened the front door and the music faded,
dying. I heard Quinn's loud voice.

"There he is!"

Tessa said, "We've been so worried."

"The weary foot soldier," Quinn said. "Home from the
front."

The famous correspondent, standing at Quinn's elbow,
laughed quietly as if at some private joke. Swig Borowy did
a little jig behind the bar. More hubbub and laughter, the
clink of ice cubes, a woman's cry, and Quinn's piano again,
a furious heartbreaking blues.

"Stay awhile," Tessa said. "Stay here. We want you to
stay with us."

I looked at Quinn. Massive in brown tweed, his back
was to me now, his head bent low over the keys. His feet

pumped the piano pedals. I observed that his shoes were polished to a glassy shine, of the cracked brilliance found only in old, very expensive, well-cared-for English leather. He was elegantly turned out, a model of an American gentleman; the beard gave him a nautical air, as if he'd just stepped off a yacht. His skin looked as well cared for as his shoes. The heavy gold watch on his wrist set off little showers of light, as his hand moved left and right, walking the dog. He exhaled and settled, lowering his head. I stepped back and suddenly it was as if a headless musician was playing the piano. From my angle of vision I saw only his broad tweed back, his polished shoes, and his glittering left hand, effortlessly restless, roving the keyboard. Quinn's portrait, his features distorted by smoke, completed the surrealism. His head appeared to be floating three feet above his body.

"Stay for Christmas," Tessa said. "We need you. We're having Christmas here together. We're going to make a wassail and a Christmas pud and a goose, then decorate the tree and exchange presents. An English Christmas with American trimmings, and we'll have a party on Boxing Day. And then it's quits for Quinn and me, we're going our separate ways. And why shouldn't we? Hasn't it been fun, though? This time together? Our carnival time. But now we're cutting our losses, we're selling short." Quinn, concentrating on the blues, did not seem to hear. His chin was on his chest, his head still out of sight. He was playing softly now, a tune I knew but could not name. It was a favorite from the old days. The others had drifted away into the dining room and now it was just Tessa and me standing at the bar, the naked green tree inconspicuous in the far corner. And of course Quinn's portrait over the piano.

I said, "She was here a minute ago."

"Where?"

"Outside," I said.

She said, "We got you into it and now we're going to get you out."

"Yes," I said, smiling. "How?"

190

She leaned close to me, talking seriously; it was a plan of campaign. They'd worked it out, she and Quinn. It had all begun so innocently and in such a spirit of fun and adventure. And Marty was willing! And you were! Quinn said that it was as if we were all millionaires, loose in the seductive north country, to the back of beyond. Our resources were without limit, however much we needed we would always have enough. We were living on the accumulated interest from wise investments. Also, he was working on his theory of the two cultures—Two! My goodness, there were always two and often as many as nine, like the lives of a cat. You know Quinn, not a man of moderation; just a little bit too much is never enough for Quinn. The question was, how much was enough for you? What was your legal limit? Just how irresponsible were you prepared—able—to be? You were a man who had gone back to the fundamentals; this was your country. You had migrated to the silent woods, close to God, where the air was clear and bracing. Except you had a last chapter that wouldn't write, the woods weren't helpful; the cold made things brittle, and the seasons were slow to change. The hills reminded you of the war, the one that had no end; or that you couldn't end. You could not end it or explain it, either one. In that way, didn't it resemble the human brain? You were too far inside it, its limits were yours; and it was in control.

She said, "So Quinn had an idea. He wanted to put you two close together and into a kind of combat, it didn't matter which kind; he wanted to know which culture was the stronger and more durable, which the path to the future and which the cul-de-sac. Those seemed to be the only choices, and what better guide than a woman met by chance, a young woman unencumbered. And you know Quinn, he loves to set out mine fields and watch people move through them. He had been away from America for so long, he did not know how things were. You were his only contact. And you were obsessed by the war. And he was so interested in your response and in hers. Was there common ground after all?

And a way to prepare for the future, postwar. And how did that connect to the past, or was it only a parenthesis? It seemed an ideal encounter, a man who came from the fundamentals and a woman who was looking for them. Then—"

"Did he find out?"

"He found out something. Not that."

"What, then?"

She smiled, lifting her glass so that it obscured her eyes. The light was bad in the living room. She made a vague gesture, as if to sweep the question away. She said, "He's a musician, and a musician's like a doctor. To produce health, a doctor must investigate disease; to produce harmony, a musician must investigate discord." She added, "I think he was surprised."

"There must be more to it than that."

"Must there? I doubt it." She thought a moment, hand to mouth. "It's quite a lot, really. It's enough. This is a secular place, remember. And it's a way of life." She lowered her voice. "He wants out of all this. It's been hard on him, composing things. He's been outside so long, it's taken its toll, more than you'd imagine, much more, and I think he's eager to get back inside, to old Plumb. That's where he's at ease, at home in his imagination. Who wouldn't be? Wouldn't you?" I recoiled and she turned suddenly, brightening. "A writer takes it one step farther, immersed in chaos in order to produce order. The life of the imagination, boom boom. And if not, where are you most comfortable and eager to get back to?" When I didn't answer—there being no answer I could think to give—she returned to the other. "He's alone now, entirely solo. And he likes it. It's his own choice, be-lieve me. So he can do what he wants, can't he?"

I said, "What do you mean, secular?"

"We don't go in for spiritual things here. We don't believe in epiphany or magic, though Quinn's music is sa-cred." She paused and we listened to Quinn. She said, "We depend on human intelligence and initiative, and we cannot accept the idea that there are no more resources. It's always been a long hard slog from one place to the next, and God doesn't come into it."

"Yes," I said. It was no different from the Zone then.

She looked at me slyly. "When did you last talk to your son?"

When was it? Yesterday? The day before? Last week? I said, "It was only yesterday."

"And he was there, in the woods?"

"Oh, yes," I said, "He lives there."

She began to ask me questions, where he was born and what he looked like and where he went to school and what he wore, his favorite sports and music and his astrological sign. Was he fond of animals? I answered the questions as best I could. He was sturdy and wore corduroys and heavy sweaters. I bought him a new pair of sneakers every three months, he was growing so fast. We had a spaniel. He was a good camper, though easily distracted. He skied and loved baseball. No, it was I who loved baseball. He loved soccer. Popular with girls. Lately we had been talking about the draft, years away for him; but he had heard about it on the evening news and was determined not to sign up. He was terrified by the military life, its danger and drabness and regimentation and drills. I said that he must, it was a citizen's duty. It was a citizen's duty to go if called, unless there were genuine religious objections. And if I'm killed? he asked me. What then? I thought of him in his heavy sweater, corduroys, and sneakers, in the sights of the hard-muscled Viet Cong. He would be skylarking, not paying attention; he knew nothing of peril, so would not be alert. He wouldn't stand a chance, in her sights. She would wait patiently for a clear shot, a moment when he was still, his head lifted to the sky. Without remorse she would rise, aim, and fire. . . .

I could not finish this thought. In my imagination the

film always stopped there, the bullet approaching my son's temple. He was laughing, the bullet a millimeter away from his skull, out of his vision. It would be there forever, but he would be unaware of it, and the world therefore would never hold terror; he would never know fear. And the answer to his last question? And if I'm killed? What then? I would reply in my father's voice, dense with experience; it was a father's responsibility to take the large-minded view. I would say that I had no answer, except that dying was sometimes a citizen's duty.

"All this," she said, gesturing expansively, indicating the bar, the sofa, the piano, the portrait, the various objects. She seemed not to have heard anything I said. The curtains were gray with the first faint light of morning, and the effect was to create a cathedral hush. "Hasn't it been something, all this? Your boy, he'll never know any of it. All this, it'll be gone by the time he's old enough."

I nodded, listening.

He'll have to do without it, she said.

I smiled. Yes, he would have to.

Thank God we had it, she said. This is the real world, right here, with the real world's rules. We had the country in the best time it's ever known. Isn't that right? She sang softly, to Quinn's music,

> . . . you're breaking my heart.
> You've changed.
> You're not the angel I once knew.
> No need to tell me that we're through.
> It's all over now.
> You've changed.

What she was getting at? If it was what I thought it was, I didn't like it. Quinn had ceased to play, was sitting quietly on his piano bench, his head still concealed. The music was still in the air, so blue; Tessa continued to hum. I took a step toward him, moving Tessa out of the way. I moved in the direction of the piano, my arms raised, deter-

194

mined to smash the instrument to bits and have done with all this and the rules of the real world.

But there was no one there at all. Quinn and Tessa had gone to bed and I was alone in a crouch, fists raised, sweating, that awful racket in my head—and the room, brightening with the morning sun, as silent as a tomb.

eleven

I went home but things were no better there so I left. I flew to New York and then to Washington, drifting, staying with friends. It took me six months to secure a visa to return to the Zone. I believed my book ended there, and only there on the ground would I find my answer to the war's ultimate questions. How had the people fared, and what was the metamorphosis of their collective memory? Were they consoled? And what was the price? Really, it was all one question.

My son and I had an emotional farewell. I returned to the woods for a weekend, and a hike on the Long Trail. I told him my journey to the Zone was a necessity, and not a beginning but an end. A period to one sentence and after the period a long pause before beginning another. The Zone, I said, was the place where modern American history begins. He looked at me doubtfully but said he understood and offered his small hand for a manly shake. This was Sunday morning and we stood on the trail above our town, ready to descend. With the glasses we could see the tin roof of our house and the steeple of the church in the town way below. We embraced awkwardly and hefted the backpacks, his almost as heavy as mine; it was warm and we were both sweating a little. We could see bits and pieces of our own trail as it wound north, then curved back on itself, then was lost altogether in the firs. To the east we could see the White Mountains.

He asked me tentatively if there was shooting still. Would I be killed? No, I said; the country was at peace, as tranquil as the blue mountains of the north country, and as safe as the Long Trail itself. Of course this was not quite the truth. I told him that in fact the two places had quite a lot in common. The look of the land was similar; the people were self-possessed in both places, and reserved with out-siders. In the south it was always warm, the heat thick and oppressive, threatening. I talked on about the weather and the terrain and the hospitality of the population; they would be hospitable now that they were no longer occupied. He stared at me expressionless, and I assured him that I spoke the truth. However, he had heard so much about the war from me that he could not credit this. He remembered eve-nings in front of the television set, the summer the capital fell. He could not recall the details, but he remembered the tense atmosphere in the living room and my loud mouth. It was my voice that scared him. How long ago was that? he asked. I told him it was years ago, another time alto-gether; things were different now. And it was no longer our affair. There were no cameramen or reporters, and not a single American soldier.

So I won't have to go there to fight?

Of course not, Jack, I said.

Daddy, he insisted. Ever?

Jack, I said. Never.

He turned away from me, adjusting the straps of his backpack. It was heavy and he bent under its weight. He looked at me warily and said, But you said I would, that I would have to register for the draft and go off to fight. He paused and moved closer, peering at me with his sweet little boy's face, and the look told me that he thought somehow that I wanted him to go to war to die, a citizen's duty. So many had died, and I spoke of them with such respect. I

seemed to love the dead more than the living. He recoiled
when I touched his shoulder. My God, I thought, what have
I done?

They could have been me, he said.

I said they could have been, but the war was over now.
Really, I pleaded, the country was at peace and there was
no danger. They had won.

He smiled, wanting to believe. But if that is so, he asked
quietly, why are you going?

◇

Ho Chi Minh City was not easy to visit. It was especially
difficult for anyone who had been there in the days of the
occupation. The present regime was suspicious of the former proconsuls. We were defeated but still dangerous, and
everyone knew the ancient proverb about the wounded elephant that turned on the starving tiger. I had to establish
my bona fides in a number of ways, some of them dishonest.
But I was clever about it and managed to convince the authorities that sympathetic news dispatches would help create a sunny climate for productive diplomacy. The authorities
were eager to re-establish relations, perhaps on the theory
that the two nations had been locked in an embrace for so
long that it was shameful and absurd that both end their
days as enemies. Also each bore a measure of responsibility
for the other. Their responsibility was to make certain we
did not forget. Ours was to repair the damage done in our
heroic effort to interfere with their revolution. Truly, they
wanted an apology.

I was quick to agree with their view. It was simple
justice, I told them, and declared that there was a great
reservoir of goodwill among the American people. The
American people harbored no bitterness. The war was past,
and Americans were quick to forgive. The American administration had to be made to see this, and in that I would be
honored to play a part.

I added that it would help—it would help *me* in the

preparation of my dispatches—if there was progress in the area of identification of the American missing. This was a large issue in America despite the commendable indifference toward the war itself, erased as it was from the public conscience. The concern with the missing men was personal. Friends and relatives of the missing men had a powerful lobby in the capital, an influence out of all proportion to their number, which was small and widely dispersed throughout the many towns and villages of the countryside. I smiled and lowered my voice. There were so many. Really, they were the American component of the Vietnamese diaspora.

There are no American missing, the official said.

An awkward moment, and I hesitated. Yes, I said finally. To be sure. Of course. But the wives, children, and parents of the lost servicemen were adamant. Obsessed, actually. They wanted verification.

That would not be possible, the official said.

Certainly, I said, it would be very difficult.

It would be impossible, the official admitted.

I understand completely, I said.

All Americans are accounted for, he said.

So I made my voyage on a two-week visa secured after many letters and interviews. Much of what I expected to find I had arranged in my mind already; it was merely a chore of finding the facts and situations to support my conclusions. That is, what had gone before; what I was seeking now was the last chapter, my summing-up. But the trip did not go well. My escort was a young woman who had been successfully re-educated and wished now to join her country's diplomatic service; she was avid to go to America, after the normalization of relations. She knew the names of the various states and regions, and professed admiration for our popular culture. She had known a number of Americans during the occupation and had found them clumsy and often cruel but guileless and generous with money; ill at ease, so far from home. Americans, she concluded, did not travel well.

She said if I wished to change my dollars for piasters, she could arrange it. There were two rates, now as before. I laughed. Some things were the same, a nice journalist's irony. In the old days the black money market had been monopolized by Indians and was known informally as the Bank of India. I asked her if the mahatma was still in business, in the crowded apartment around the corner from the Caravelle Hotel.

She looked at me coldly. "His name is Mr. Nguyen," she said.

We traveled here and there in an official car, and I might have been the only foreign visitor. We saw no other Caucasians, though there were rumors of delegations from East Germany and Austria also touring the countryside. I had drawn up an itinerary but it was ignored, there being many locations still off limits; I was not allowed anywhere near the Cambodian border, or the border with Laos. I made a list of military officials I wished to see, but they, too, were unavailable. We traveled mostly in the Delta and saw little evidence of the war, except for the presence of American vehicles—Jeeps, trucks, armored personnel carriers, tanks, and bulldozers. There were as many as a dozen interviews a day with cadre, managers of small factories and co-op markets and orphanages. Local authorities sat in on the meetings, polite but also alert. The interviews told me nothing I wanted to know. I made detailed notes but knew they were unusable. The country seemed so much more mysterious with no Americans in it. It seemed like a different state altogether and, without my countrymen, inscrutable. I realized then how much I had depended on the Americans for my news. Even the lies and misapprehensions were American, rising from the American character and obedient to it; the history was American. Surely the Vietnamese embraced lies and misapprehensions as gaudy and exotic as our own, but I did not know what they were. Their jinns were not mine. I had grown comfortable inside the American illusion and could not comprehend the Vietnamese, so it was hopeless weighing and measuring today against yesterday. There was no connection between them. I began to think of the war as a parenthesis inside a far-going sentence, the parenthesis in English but the sentence itself in a language I did not know and could not decipher. I understood finally that I was on my own.

After a week of travel I fell ill and we returned to Ho Chi Minh City. The doctor gave me antibiotics and a tranquilizer and I went to bed. I wrote many letters home to my son and abroad to Quinn and to Tessa. Each day I sent a postcard to Marty, a panorama of the city in primary colors. My messages to her were always light and cheerful, though somewhat impersonal, as if I were writing a news dispatch. In the morning and again in the evening my escort visited me, bringing translations of various documents, speeches, white papers, agricultural plans, assorted balance sheets. I accepted these with thanks and put them away in the bureau unread.

One night she arrived with tea from the restaurant. She sat on the edge of the bed and reminisced about her former life, her collection of Beatles records, her Honda, and afternoons around the swimming pool of the Cercle Sportif. Her father, now dead, had been a junior minister in the puppet administration and her mother owned a business. She used to watch COMUSMACV play tennis with the commander of Military Region Three. At noon the ambassador would take his swim, six consecutive lengths of the pool; no more, no less. There had been a German correspondent who made passes at her. He wore tight swimming trunks and left his wife to come over to speak to her at poolside. She had always been polite but conscious of the wife twenty paces away. The swimming trunks had revealed his sex. His wife had watched them as they talked. This was not correct, was it?

No, I said.

He was a common German, she said. I used to see you there, too.

Not likely, I said. It was someone else. I was rarely at the Cercle Sportif.

She laughed and described the woman I was with. She then gave her name, a charming mispronunciation.

You have me at a disadvantage, I said.

We thought you were a spy, she replied.

I laughed. No, my concern was with the news only. The German was the spy.

The one with the sex?

Yes, I said.

For which side? she asked. By and by she looked at me with a thin pretty smile, excusing herself and rising to go to the bathroom. She was fluid and delicate in her movements, her silk *ao dai* swishing as she opened the door and closed it. There was silence for a few moments and then I heard the shower; then she was bending over me, turning out the light. I had not been with a woman for a very long time and was conscious of my rough skin against hers. She was so tiny and fragile, yet in the dim light from the square her skin looked polished and heavy as marble. We embraced for a long moment and I felt clumsy and incompetent, lacking in subtlety. I admitted this and she said it was owing to my illness, and the confusion of visiting a people's republic. Illness and alienation took many forms and this was one of them. Hers was a special country and not everyone adapted to it. She said she could help and I encouraged her but kept losing my way. It was as if I had forgotten something I wanted very much to remember, an ordinary obvious thing that eluded me. Her arms were like steel around my back, but I could not respond. In any event, I didn't. It was alarming, like losing the tune of a well-loved song or the point of a story. She was so affectionate and forceful. We stayed in bed together a long time, talking; then she slept for a while. and when she woke she left.

I was content in my bed at the Caravelle, watching the activity in Lam Son Square. I wrote my letters late at night and the concierge mailed them for me. I assumed they were read and censored but did not care, and in any case I had no comment to make on the nature of things now. They were unknowable, perhaps better not known. I related stories about the essence of things then. To Tessa and to Quinn I attempted to relate the facts of the situation in the Zone to life at Chester Square. They were both in their separate ways parenthetical and without obvious links to what had gone before and what would come after. They seemed to exist for their own sake alone and for what they could teach others, and for the emotion involved. Nothing more to be made of them, except their incomprehensibility once experienced. Of course that, too, was a judgment of sorts. The more intense the experience, the less articulate the expression.

But I had made a discovery, and this I confided to my friend the diplomat after deciding it would not be welcome to Quinn. It was the only letter I wrote to the diplomat, and I sent it care of the Department of State; the post was unreliable in his country of residence. I suspected he would find my discovery incoherent and sentimental, and no doubt a violation of the physicist's natural law, but I wanted to tell him, anyway.

I wrote him this. For many years I had accepted the thesis, half a century old now, that the large abstract words such as glory, honor, courage, and cowardice, were obscene. That which was chaste was factual, in the instance of the war, the details of the weather, the geography, the weapons, the battle groups, and the statistical apparatus that supported it all. Now I knew I was mistaken and in this war all we had were the large abstract words. It was difficult to state them without mortification, but I had a skull filled to overflowing with facts—untainted, innocent—and none of them described the war, except who had won and who had lost and in this war that was only a detail.

Only the large words were equal to the experience, in which the sacrifice was so out of balance and the results so confounding. Glory or disgrace, sacred or profane; pick the words you want. Only in this way would the deepest secrets, those closest to the heart, be disclosed. They were the only secrets worth disclosing. The times were so noisy and the people so distracted, it was certain this message would go unheard. There was so much at stake and so much lost, the crimes so numerous and the surveillance so shallow, the honor so elusive—final chapters and grand endings were inherently suspect, as the last breath of discredited romanticism. But sooner or later the war would have to be seen whole and in daylight, or else. *Amerikanische Kunst des 20. Jahrhunderts.*

◊

I wrote my letters in the evenings, in longhand, propped up in bed, feverish, drugged, always thirsty. I wrote by the milky light of the lamps in Lam Son Square, listening to cassettes of Tatum and Billie Holiday and Ella Fitzgerald and Fats. I saw ghosts in the shadows; it seemed to me that multitudes were gathering beneath my window, waiting for a signal to mobilize. What a mighty army they would be, free at last. I rose from my bed and made my way onto the balcony to stand, my hands gripping the railing, sweating in the damp heat of the dark early morning, vigilant. The jungle was closing in. There was no movement anywhere, no cars, no far-off explosions, no drunken laughter, not even a bicycle or rat. The silence was complete, except for the music behind me; there was no living thing in sight, only the tortured shadows of the past crowding my memory.

I never slept, so it was that way each night. I rose and stepped to the balcony, watching and listening. I stood naked, sweating, hearing only the restless racket inside my own mind, and the blues on tape. How could I communicate this in a personal letter? You wouldn't understand. My imagined multitudes held me in thrall, and I would not banish them. They were necessary. They were close as brothers, my multitudes; they were mine.

I moved forward into the heat. The railing looked fragile, ready to give way at the slightest touch. A sudden breeze froze the sweat on my skin and I began to shiver. I watched and listened, as anyone does in the darkness, but did not venture beyond the balcony. Do you see it now? I was so tired, and in order to advance I would have to travel through the multitudes, from the present into the past, counting, weighing, measuring, *listening*. They had given so much and wanted so little in return; they only wanted an acknowledgment of the debt. They wanted a secure place in the public memory. None of us must be forgotten, and in that way the future is guaranteed and our sleep untroubled. So we must ask for mercy, and it was in the *asking* . . .

Listen, I said. Everything's going to work out fine.